— YOU ARE —

Never Alone

Trust in the Miracle of
GOD'S PRESENCE *and* POWER

STUDY GUIDE | SIX SESSIONS

MAX LUCADO

THOMAS NELSON
Since 1798

Published in Nashville, Tennessee, by Thomas Nelson. Thomas Nelson is a registered trademark of HarperCollins Christian Publishing, Inc.

Published in association with Anvil II Management, Inc.

All Scripture quotations, unless otherwise noted, are taken from the Holy Bible, New International Version®. NIV®. Copyright 1973, 1978, 1984, 2011 by Biblica, Inc.® Used by permission. All rights reserved worldwide.

Scripture quotations marked ESV are taken from The Holy Bible, English Standard Version®. ESV® Text Edition: 2016. Copyright © 2001 by Crossway, a publishing ministry of Good News Publishers. The ESV® text has been reproduced in cooperation with and by permission of Good News Publishers. Unauthorized reproduction of this publication is prohibited. All rights reserved.

Scripture quotations marked MSG are taken from THE MESSAGE, copyright © 1993, 2002, 2018 by Eugene H. Peterson. Used by permission of NavPress. All rights reserved. Represented by Tyndale House Publishers, Inc.

Scripture quotations marked NCV are taken from the New Century Version®. Copyright © 2005 by Thomas Nelson. Used by permission. All rights reserved.

Scripture quotations marked NLT are taken from the *Holy Bible*, New Living Translation, copyright © 1996, 2004, 2015 by Tyndale House Foundation. Used by permission of Tyndale House Publishers, Inc., Carol Stream, Illinois 60188. All rights reserved.

Scripture quotations marked NKJV are taken from the New King James Version®. Copyright © 1982 by Thomas Nelson. Used by permission. All rights reserved.

Thomas Nelson titles may be purchased in bulk for educational, business, fundraising, or sales promotional use. For information, please e-mail SpecialMarkets@ThomasNelson.com.

ISBN 978-0-310-11555-7 (softcover)
ISBN 978-0-310-11556-4 (ebook)

First Printing August 2020 / Printed in the United States of America

Contents

A Word from
Max Lucado

Mother Teresa once said, "The most terrible poverty is loneliness, and the feeling of being unloved." Perhaps you are acquainted with this kind of poverty in your life. You are familiar with the downward spiral. You have convinced yourself no one cares, no one can help you, no one can hear you, and no one can heed your call. You feel inside that you are on your own.

Well, if you know this feeling, I want to tell you that you aren't alone. I don't mean you aren't alone in *knowing* the feeling. I mean that you *literally* aren't alone. That raw, dark sense of isolation and powerlessness? It isn't here to stay.

If you're not convinced, I have some stories for you to consider. Actually, the disciple John has some stories for you to consider. He interwove a tapestry of miracles in his Gospel so you can know that you are never truly on your own when Jesus is in your life. In John's own words, he wrote about these miracles so "you may believe that Jesus is the Messiah, the Son of God, and that by believing you may have life in his name" (John 20:31).

Life-giving belief! This is what John wants you to experience. Abundant, robust, and resilient faith. John wants you to understand that life happens when you *believe*. You find strength beyond your strength. You accomplish tasks beyond your capacity. You discover solutions beyond your wisdom. Belief happens when you place your confidence in God.

As you do, you have "life in his name." This is the purpose of the miracles that John records! He recounts these signs to stir conviction in this promise: *you are never, ever, alone*. Was this not one of the final promises of Christ? Before he ascended to heaven, he assured his friends, "I am with you always, to the end of the age" (Matthew 28:20 ESV).

Those words meant everything to John. At the time he wrote his Gospel, he was an aged apostle serving a church in the city of Ephesus. Hair silver. Skin wrinkled. He is the last of the original disciples of Christ. Peter, Andrew, James, and the rest are all gone. Only John remains—and he knows his days are coming to an end. So he takes up one final task.

Mark's Gospel is in circulation. Matthew and Luke have compiled their accounts. But John's Gospel will be different. He will tell stories the others didn't tell and add details to the ones they did relate. He will structure his Gospel around a cross-section of "signs."

First, John takes us to Cana to sample some wine. Then he takes us to Capernaum to watch a father embrace a son he feared would die. We feel the fury of an angry storm in Galilee and hear the murmur of a hungry crowd on a hillside. We watch a paralytic stand up and a blind man look up. Before John is done, he leads us through two cemeteries, near one cross, and invites us to eavesdrop on a breakfast chat that forever changed the life of an apostle.

John's intention in relating these miracles is not to serve as entries in a history book but as samples from God's playbook. He recorded them not to impress you but to urge you to believe in the tender presence and mighty power of Christ. This montage of miracles proclaims: *God's got this!* Think it's all up to you? Hogwash. God will carry you. You're stronger than you think because God is nearer than you know.

Had Jesus just wanted to make a case for his divinity, he could have materialized a flock of birds out of thin air, caused trees to uproot, turned creeks into waterfalls, or transformed rocks into bumblebees. Such deeds would have demonstrated his power. But he wanted you to see *more.* He wanted to show you a miracle-working God who loves you, cares for you, and comes to your aid. And don't you need to know this message today?

When life seems depleted . . . does God care?

When I'm facing an onslaught of challenges . . . will God help?

When life grows dark and stormy . . . will God be there?

The answer in the life-giving miracles in the Gospel of John is a resounding *yes.*

Do you know these miracles? Do you believe in a Jesus who not only has power but also a passionate love for the weak and wounded of the world? Do you think he cares enough about you to find you in the lonely waiting rooms, rehab centers, and convalescent homes of life? Do you desire to know the God who will meet you in the midst of life's messes?

If so, take a good look at the words of John and the miracles of Christ and see if they don't achieve their desired goal: "That you may believe that Jesus is the Messiah, the Son of God, and that by believing you may have life in his name" (John 20:31).

How to Use This Guide

The *You Are Never Alone Video Study* is designed to be experienced in a group setting such as a Bible study, Sunday school class, or any small group gathering. Each session begins with a brief opening reflection and icebreaker questions to get you and your group thinking about the topic. You will then watch a video with Max Lucado and jump into some directed small-group discussion. You will close each session with a time of prayer.

Each person in the group should have his or her own study guide, which includes video teaching notes, Bible study and group discussion questions, and between-sessions personal studies to help you reflect and apply the material to your life during the week. You are also encouraged to have a copy of the *You Are Never Alone* book, as reading it alongside the curriculum will provide you with deeper insights and make the journey more meaningful. See the "recommended reading" section at the end of each session for the chapters in the book that correspond to the material you and your group are discussing.

To get the most out of your group experience, keep the following points in mind. First, the real growth in this study will happen during your small-group time. This is where you will process the content of Max's message, ask questions, and learn from others as you hear what God is doing in their lives. For this reason, it is important for you to be fully committed to the group and attend each session so you can build trust and rapport with the other members. If you choose to only "go through the motions," or if you refrain from participating, there is a lesser chance you will find what you're looking for during this study.

Second, remember that the goal of your small group is to serve as a place where people can share, learn about God, and build intimacy and friendship. For this reason, seek to make your group a "safe place." This means being honest about your thoughts and feelings and listening carefully to everyone else's opinion. (If you are a group leader, there are additional instructions and resources in the back of the book for leading a productive discussion group.)

Third, resist the temptation to "fix" a problem someone might be having or to correct his or her theology, as that's not the purpose of your small-group time. Also, keep everything your group shares confidential. This will foster a rewarding sense of community in your group and create a place where people can heal, be challenged, and grow spiritually.

Following your group time, maximize the impact of the course with the additional between-sessions studies. For each session, you may wish to complete the personal study all in one sitting or spread it out over a few days (for example, working on it a half-hour a day on several different days that week). Note that if you are unable to finish (or even start!) your between-sessions personal study, you should still attend the group study video session. You are still wanted and welcome at the group even if you don't have your "homework" done.

Keep in mind this study is an opportunity for you to train in a new way of seeing yourself and your walk with God. The videos, discussions, and activities are simply meant to kick-start your imagination so you are not only open to what God wants you to hear but also how to apply it to your life. As you read the miracles related in John's Gospel, be listening to what God has to say to you through his Word and be reassured in his promise that *you are never alone.*

God Is with You in the Ordinary

On the third day a wedding took place at Cana in Galilee. Jesus' mother was there, and Jesus and his disciples had also been invited to the wedding. When the wine was gone, Jesus' mother said to him, "They have no more wine." "Woman, why do you involve me?" Jesus replied. "My hour has not yet come." His mother said to the servants, "Do whatever he tells you."

JOHN 2:1–5

WELCOME

What was the last request you made to God? Was it for something big? Something small? Have you ever caught yourself apologizing to God for your requests?

"I know you might not care about this . . ."

"I know this doesn't really matter in the grand scheme of things . . ."

"I know this seems like such a silly request . . ."

Why do we do this? Why are we so hesitant to pray for the "small things" in life? Perhaps it has to do with how we view God. We see him as holy and distant. Someone far off and far above everything happening on earth. We don't view him as near and present, involved in our everyday lives, or moving through the world in an intimate way.

John opens his Gospel with the statement, "In the beginning was the Word, and the Word was with God, and the Word was God" (1:1). John tells us the *Word* is Jesus, "the only begotten of the Father, full of grace and truth," and that he "became flesh and made his dwelling among us" (verse 14). Jesus was God-in-the-flesh. Once Jesus ascended into heaven, he left us with his Spirit (see 2 Corinthians 5:5)—a guide who, like the air around you, is everywhere, and like the breath in your lungs, is inside you.

So, if God is as near as your own breath, surely he is aware of what is happening in your life, in your mind, in your heart, and in your body. Furthermore, he is *concerned* about the details of your life—in your mind, heart, and body. He is with you in the highest of highs and deepest of lows. He is with you just as much during a trip to the supermarket as he is when you're heading to the hospital for a checkup. He is in the ordinary moments of life.

In this opening session, we will look at Jesus' first miracle recorded in John. It happened as a result of an ordinary problem in an ordinary setting and involved ordinary materials. Jesus didn't heal anyone, or miraculously feed thousands, or even offer any parables or other teaching. Yet John recorded the story just as he did all the others—which means this story can tell us something important about who Jesus was and what that means for our lives today.

So today, find comfort in this Jesus who was divine yet altogether ordinary. This man who woke up each day, worked, fished, drank water and, occasionally, turned it into wine.

SHARE

If you or any of your group members don't know each other, take a few minutes to introduce yourselves. Then, to get things started, discuss one of the following questions.

- Do you ever wonder if your prayer requests are too small for God? If so, why do you think that is the case?

  — or —

- What is your prayer style? Do you pray to God spontaneously, read prayers written by others, or some other method? Who taught you to pray this way?

READ

Invite someone to read the following verses aloud. Listen for fresh insights as you hear the verses being read, and then discuss the questions that follow.

[6] Are not five sparrows sold for two pennies? Yet not one of them is forgotten by God. [7] Indeed, the very hairs of your head are all numbered. Don't be afraid; you are worth more than many sparrows (Luke 12:6–7).

Do not be anxious about anything, but in every situation, by prayer and petition, with thanksgiving, present your requests to God (Philippians 4:6).

Give all your worries and cares to God, for he cares about you (1 Peter 5:7 NLT).

What is one key insight that stands out to you from these passages?

According to these verses, what does God care about when it comes to your life?

WATCH

Play the video segment for session one. As you watch, use the following outline to record any thoughts or concepts that stand out to you.

John wrote down the miracles that he presents in his Gospel not to impress us but to urge us to believe in the presence of Christ.

When we believe in Jesus, we have *life* . . . abundant, robust, and resilient life. We find strength beyond our strength. We accomplish tasks beyond our capacity. We see solutions beyond our wisdom. And we realize we are never, ever, alone.

As far as miracles go, bone-dry wine vats at a wedding don't even tip the scale. But perhaps this is actually the point: the *ordinariness* of it all. God wants us to come to him with our requests in *everything*—not just the big things of life.

Mary didn't worry that the size of her request was too small. She simply connected the problem with the provider. The result was miraculous provision and restoration of what had been lost.

Mary's demonstration of faith caught Jesus' attention. Not only that, but it changed his agenda.

A precise prayer gives Jesus the opportunity to remove all doubt about his love. Your problem becomes his pathway. The challenge you face becomes a canvas on which he can demonstrate his finest work.

DISCUSS

Take a few minutes with your group members to discuss what you just watched and explore these concepts in Scripture.

1. John writes toward the end of his Gospel, "These [stories] are written that you may believe that Jesus is the Messiah, the Son of God, and that by believing you may have life in his name" (John 20:31). What does this tell you about John's purpose in recording Jesus' miracles? What does it mean to "have life in his name"?

2. John starts things off in his Gospel with a sign from Christ that seems . . . *ordinary*. What situation prompted this miracle? What was the "crisis" at hand?

3. What request did Mary make of Jesus? Why do you think Jesus was hesitant at first to answer her request?

4. How did Mary respond to Jesus when he said, "My hour has not yet come" (John 2:4)? Why do you think she responded this way? What happened as a result?

5. Have you ever prayed for something specific and did not receive it? If so, how did you respond? Why do you think God withheld what you wanted?

6. John writes, "What Jesus did here in Cana of Galilee was the first of the signs through which he revealed his glory; and his disciples believed in him" (verse 11). Who believed in Jesus after this miracle? Why is this significant?

7. What caused *you* to believe in Jesus? How did that moment, event, or person convince you? Or, if you don't believe in Christ, what *would* make you believe?

8. What is something new or interesting you learned from Jesus' miracle of turning water to wine? How could this apply to your everyday life and your everyday faith?

RESPOND

Spend a few moments in silence contemplating Philippians 4:6, which you read at the beginning of this session: "Do not be anxious about anything, but in every situation, by prayer and petition, with thanksgiving, present your requests to God." Use the space below to write down two or three requests you want to make known to God right now.

CLOSE

Spend some time sharing prayer requests with one another. You can share a request you wrote above or a different one. Remember, no request is too small for God! Have one person write down requests as you are sharing. End your time together by praying briefly for each request. You can either take turns praying or one person can lead the group in prayer.

Between-Sessions
Personal Study

Reflect on the material you've covered this week by engaging in any or all of the following between-sessions activities. (Before you begin, you may want to read chapter 2 in *You Are Never Alone*.) Each personal study consists of several reflection activities to help you implement what you learned in the group time. The time you invest will be well spent, so let God use it to draw you closer to him. At your next meeting, share any key points or insights that stood out to you as you spent this time with the Lord.

DO YOU BELIEVE IN MIRACLES?

This study is all about the miracles of Jesus and why they matter for us today. Given this, before you go through the next few weeks of study, it's important to consider how you feel about the miracles recorded in the Bible. Honestly consider your thoughts, beliefs, and opinions as you work through today's personal study. Answer the following questions to get you started.

1. Have you ever personally experienced a miracle or witnessed a miracle take place in someone else's life? If so, what was that experience like for you? If not, would you say you still believe in miracles? Why or why not?

2. What has informed your belief in the area of miracles—your faith, the faith of your parents, or beliefs you have heard others express? Explain your answer.

3. How do you feel about the miracles described in the Bible? Do you believe they happened or do you consider them folklore? Explain your response.

4. When Paul wrote letters to the early church, he was careful to remind his readers that Jesus was fully human but also fully God, as the following passages relate:

    ⁹ For in Christ all the fullness of the Deity lives in bodily form, and in Christ you have been brought to

fullness. [10] He is the head over every power and authority (Colossians 2:9-10).

[5] For there is one God and one mediator between God and mankind, the man Christ Jesus, [6] who gave himself as a ransom for all people (1 Timothy 2:5-6).

[5] In your relationships with one another, have the same mindset as Christ Jesus: [6] Who, being in very nature God, did not consider equality with God something to be used to his own advantage; [7] rather, he made himself nothing by taking the very nature of a servant, being made in human likeness (Philippians 2:5-7).

How is Jesus described in each of these passages? What are some of the key characteristics that Paul points out about Jesus?

5. Considering your answers to the previous question, how would you describe Jesus? As God? As man? As both? Explain your answer.

6. How can an understanding of who Jesus actually was affect the way you view the miracles he performed and whether or not you believe in them?

Prayer: *Assess how you feel after today's study. Did these questions stir up anything in you, whether good or bad? Perhaps you have more questions for God than before. Perhaps you feel steadier in your faith than before. However you are feeling, and whatever questions you are asking, spend the next few minutes bringing them before God in prayer. You don't have to hide your doubt or skepticism or fears. Bring your full self before God's throne and listen for his voice.*

WATER TO WINE

In this week's group discussion, you looked at the story of Jesus' first miracle at Cana:

> [1] On the third day there was a wedding in Cana of Galilee, and the mother of Jesus was there. [2] Now both Jesus and His disciples were invited to the wedding. [3] And when they ran out of wine, the mother of Jesus said to Him, "They have no wine."
>
> [4] Jesus said to her, "Woman, what does your concern have to do with Me? My hour has not yet come."
>
> [5] His mother said to the servants, "Whatever He says to you, do it."

⁶ Now there were set there six waterpots of stone, according to the manner of purification of the Jews, containing twenty or thirty gallons apiece. ⁷ Jesus said to them, "Fill the waterpots with water." And they filled them up to the brim. ⁸ And He said to them, "Draw some out now, and take it to the master of the feast." And they took it. ⁹ When the master of the feast had tasted the water that was made wine, and did not know where it came from (but the servants who had drawn the water knew), the master of the feast called the bridegroom. ¹⁰ And he said to him, "Every man at the beginning sets out the good wine, and when the guests have well drunk, then the inferior. You have kept the good wine until now!"

¹¹ This beginning of signs Jesus did in Cana of Galilee, and manifested His glory; and His disciples believed in Him. (John 2:1–11 NJKV)

1. John states that Jesus and his disciples were invited to a wedding (see verse 2). What does this indicate about Jesus' social life? What does it tell you about who Jesus is?

2. At one point, Mary turned to Jesus and told him there was no wine left (see verse 3). Why do you think Mary chose to make this particular statement to Jesus? What does this tell you about the way that Mary viewed Christ?

3. As you discussed this week, the closest English translation of Jesus' words in John 2:4 appear to be, "Mother, your concern and mine are not the same." It is as if Jesus carried an "appointment book" and had a specific time in mind when he planned to reveal his power to the world—and this day in Cana was not that moment. Given this information, what does it tell you about Jesus that he decided to do the miracle anyway?

4. There were six waterpots at the wedding, each holding twenty to thirty gallons. This means that Jesus turned 120 to 180 gallons of water into wine. What is significant about the fact that Jesus provided this much abundance in performing the miracle? What does this say about the way he provides for you when you come to him with your requests?

5. How does John describe the quality of the wine (see verse 10)? What does the quality of the wine tell you about Jesus, his generosity, and his power?

6. What is something you learned about Jesus in this story? Did this story make you view Jesus in a new way? If so, how?

Prayer: *John opens his Gospel with a beautiful depiction of who Jesus was from the beginning of creation until he came to earth. Read John 1:1–4 and 14 as your prayer time today. Read the verses slowly and as many times as you want. Note that "the Word" refers to Christ himself.*

GOD IN YOUR ORDINARY

The miracle at the wedding in Cana was not a healing, a deliverance, or a resurrection. Jesus simply *turned water to wine.* An incredible feat . . . but what was the point? Compared to Jesus' other miracles, this one accomplished something quite ordinary. But as you discussed this week, this is perhaps the point: *the ordinariness of it all.* Today, spend some time studying and reflecting on how God interacts with you in your ordinary and everyday life.

1. Has God ever answered a "big request" in your life? Has he ever answered a "small request"? If so, what were your requests? How did God answer?

2. John writes, "This is the confidence we have in approaching God: that if we ask *anything* according to his will, he hears us. And if we know that he hears us—whatever we ask—we know that we have what we asked of him" (1 John 5:14–15, emphasis added). In the space below, list major problems that are causing you anxiety in the column

labeled "Big." List small problems that are causing you anxiety in the column labeled "Small."

BIG	SMALL

3. Which items on your lists have you recently brought before God in prayer? Which ones have you not prayed for yet? Why?

4. Something that sets Christianity apart from other religions is the intimacy that God has with his people. From the Old Testament to the New Testament, God is portrayed as involved, near, and present—not cold or distant. As we have seen, God was so involved with his creation that he came to dwell among us in the form of Jesus. This gives us hope that God truly cares about the ordinary parts of our lives, and we can bring anything before him. Jesus said the following in one of his teachings:

> 7 "Ask and it will be given to you; seek and you will find; knock and the door will be opened to you. 8 For everyone who asks receives; the one who seeks finds; and to the one who knocks, the door will be opened. Which of you, if your son asks for bread, will give him a stone? 10 Or if he asks for a fish, will give him a snake? 11 If you, then, though you are evil, know how to give good gifts to your children, how much more will your Father in heaven give good gifts to those who ask him! 12 So in everything, do to others what you would have them do to you, for this sums up the Law and the Prophets" (Matthew 7:7–12).

What happens when you ask, seek, and knock (see verse 7)? What types of requests does this cover? What is significant about that fact?

5. What metaphor does Jesus use to describe your Father in heaven (see verses 9–10)? How does this help you understand what God is like and how he cares for you?

6. This passage ends with a verse that is often referred to as the Golden Rule: "So in everything, do to others what you would have them do to you" (verse 12). This might seem out of place, but how do Jesus' words in verses 7–11 support this idea?

Prayer: *Read this prayer aloud or silently to yourself: "God, make me aware of your presence today. Allow me to hear your voice while I work, spend time with friends, do chores, or take care of my family. I confess I don't always believe you care about the regular moments of my life, but I need help even in the smallest things, such as my attitude, energy level, patience, and work. Remind me to surrender every fear and anxiety to you, no matter how small it is. Thank you for caring about me and the ordinary parts of my life. Thank you for being a good Father." As you go about your day, involve God in your ordinary life and tasks. Ask for small things and big things. Pay attention to his presence and what he might be saying to you.*

FURTHER REFLECTION

Reflect on what you studied this week: miracles, the character of Christ, and God's involvement in your everyday life. Journal your thoughts or write them as a prayer to God, either asking him questions about what you learned, thanking him for what you learned, or seeking answers from him on what to do next now that you better understand these topics in Scripture. Also write down any observations or questions that you want to bring to your next group time.

For Next Week: In preparation for next week, read chapters 3–4 in *You Are Never Alone*.

God Is with You When You're Stuck

Now there is in Jerusalem near the Sheep Gate a pool. . . .
One who was there had been an invalid for thirty-eight years.
When Jesus saw him lying there and learned that he had been in this
condition for a long time, he asked him, "Do you want to get well?"

JOHN 5:2, 5–6

WELCOME

Writer's block. The "glass ceiling." A fork in the road. A tire in the mud. Everyone knows what it feels like to be stuck. Stuck in a rut . . . stuck at home . . . stuck in a hospital bed . . . stuck in a dead-end job. It's a helpless and hopeless feeling.

Perhaps you can relate. Maybe you're at the end of your rope. You're out of options, resources, and patience. You're trying to get out of a tough situation, but everything you've tried hasn't worked. Or perhaps you're stuck because you just don't know what action to take. Or maybe—and this one is hard to admit—you don't *want* to take action because you've gotten comfortable in your stuck-ness. It has become comfortable for you . . . predictable. And what would happen if you got *unstuck*? The prospect is more unnerving than exciting.

Today, we will look at two different miracles that John relates in his Gospel. In each story, the recipient was stuck. One had done everything he could to get help for his dying son. The other had been unable to walk for thirty-eight years. Both of their circumstances seemed unlikely to change. Yet this did not deter Jesus. As is the case with all of his miracles, he was not satisfied to simply heal the physical needs presented to him. He went straight to the heart.

Where do you find yourself today? Are you stuck because you're at the end of your rope? Or stuck because you're afraid of what healing would look like? Either way, Jesus accepts you. He wants you to come to him with your problems. He wants to help get you unstuck no matter the reason you were stuck in the first place. But know that he won't leave it there. Our God is in the business of changing and softening hearts to become more like his.

This isn't always an easy process. Every surgery requires recovery time. Every wound requires stitches. But rest assured that when you are in the hands of the Healer, the healing is gentle and complete. No wound is left untended. No heart is left broken.

SHARE

If you or any of your group members are just meeting for the first time, take a few minutes to introduce yourselves and share any insights you have from last week's personal study.

Next, to get things started for the group time, discuss one of the following questions:

- What area of your life do you feel stuck in today? If you're not currently stuck, can you remember a time in your past when you did feel this way?

— *or* —

- When you find that you are stuck in an area of your life, what are some of your strategies for getting unstuck?

READ

Invite someone to read the following passage aloud. Listen for fresh insights as you hear the verses being read, and then discuss the questions that follow.

[1] Now there was a Pharisee, a man named Nicodemus who was a member of the Jewish ruling council. [2] He came to Jesus at night and said, "Rabbi, we know that you are a teacher who has come from God. For no one could perform the signs you are doing if God were not with him."

[3] Jesus replied, "Very truly I tell you, no one can see the kingdom of God unless they are born again."

[4] "How can someone be born when they are old?" Nicodemus asked. "Surely they cannot enter a second time into their mother's womb to be born!"

[5] Jesus answered, "Very truly I tell you, no one can enter the kingdom of God unless they are born of

water and the Spirit. [6] Flesh gives birth to flesh, but the Spirit gives birth to spirit. [7] You should not be surprised at my saying, 'You must be born again.' [8] The wind blows wherever it pleases. You hear its sound, but you cannot tell where it comes from or where it is going. So it is with everyone born of the Spirit."

[9] "How can this be?" Nicodemus asked.

[10] "You are Israel's teacher," said Jesus, "and do you not understand these things? [11] Very truly I tell you, we speak of what we know, and we testify to what we have seen, but still you people do not accept our testimony. [12] I have spoken to you of earthly things and you do not believe; how then will you believe if I speak of heavenly things?" (John 3:1–12).

What is one key insight that stands out to you from this passage?

This story takes place after Jesus turned the water into wine at Cana and before the miracle we will examine today. How did Jesus reveal that Nicodemus was "stuck" in his thinking?

WATCH

Play the video segment for session two. As you watch, use the following outline to record any thoughts or concepts that stand out to you.

The road between supplication and celebration can be a wearisome trek. Uninvited companions like despair can hitch a ride with you. They make you desperate for an answer.

Jesus was instructing the man to take him at his word and trust that the prayer offered in Cana would be answered in Capernaum. Jesus was asking him to *believe*.

Jesus' miracle was not just in giving life to the boy. The life-giving healing of the boy was a *temporary* gift. But the faith-giving miracle to the family was *eternal*.

When Jesus saw the man beside the pool, he asked, "Would you like to get well?"(John 5:6, NLT). It's an odd question. Why would Jesus ask this question? Our only clue is that the man had been ill for a long time. It was the duration of the illness that caused Jesus to pose the question.

Are you ready to take that long trek from Cana to Capernaum? If so, hear the words that Jesus said to this man by the pool: "Stand up, pick up your mat, and walk!" (John 5:8 NLT).

The God of the Bible is a God of forward motion. He is ready to write a new chapter in your biography. But he will demand that you take action to *live out* that new chapter.

DISCUSS

Take a few minutes with your group members to discuss what you just watched and explore these concepts in Scripture.

1. John writes about two men who needed a miracle: the official from Capernaum and the sick man by the pool of Bethesda. Both men were stuck, but for different reasons.

What were those reasons? How have you ever felt stuck in similar ways?

2. How do you think the official was feeling when he pleaded for Jesus to heal his son? Have you ever been in a similarly desperate situation? Who did you turn to for help?

3. How did Jesus respond to the man? How did the man respond to Jesus? Why do you think the man *believed* Jesus?

4. Who was ultimately healed in this miracle? What does this say about the purpose of Jesus' miracles?

5. The man beside the Pool of Bethesda had been sick for thirty-eight years. What is the longest period of time you have felt stuck in a bad situation? What were the causes?

6. How did the duration of your circumstances—whether due to an illness, bad job, empty bank account, or other reason—affect your motivation to get unstuck?

7. How do you feel about Jesus' question: "Do you want to get well?" (John 5:6). What do you think Jesus was getting the man to realize by asking the question?

8. Consider an area of your life in which you feel stuck today. How do you think you became stuck? What fears and questions coincide with getting unstuck?

RESPOND

Take a few minutes to list practical steps you could take to get unstuck from a situation where you feel trapped. Keep in mind that shame and guilt are not good motivators for change. Be kind with yourself as you think of actions you can handle today and in the days to come.

CLOSE

End your time together in prayer. If you need specific prayer for an area in your life where you feel stuck, share it with the group so they can pray for you. Pray for God's wisdom to know what steps you can take to get unstuck and ask for his grace in the process.

Between-Sessions
Personal Study

Reflect on the material you've covered this week by engaging in any or all of the following between-sessions activities. Each personal study consists of several reflection activities to help you implement what you learned in the group time. The time you invest will be well spent, so let God use it to draw you closer to him. At your next meeting, share any key points or insights that stood out to you as you spent this time with the Lord.

THE ROAD FROM CANA TO CAPERNAUM

In your group time this week, you looked first at John's story of the healing of an official's son. The official had traveled from his hometown of Capernaum to Cana, where Jesus was located, to ask him for a miracle. Jesus told the official, "Go back home. Your son will live!" (John 4:50 NLT). Such good news . . . but the man had wanted Jesus to come back *with him* to Capernaum. Instead, the official had to return alone, trusting his son would indeed live.

1. How would you have felt as you took that journey? Hopeful, afraid, skeptical? Why?

2. Why do you think Jesus performed this miracle as he did—by not returning with the man? Why do you think we sometimes have to wait before we get unstuck?

3. The Bible is full of stories of people who waited on the Lord for a miracle. Abraham and Sarah waited for a son (see Genesis 21). Joseph waited to be let out of prison (see Genesis 41). The Israelites waited to enter into the Promised Land (see Joshua 3). Elizabeth waited on a child (see Luke 1). There must be a purpose for all of this waiting in Scripture! Read the story of the official one more time:

46 There was a government official in nearby Capernaum whose son was very sick. 47 When he heard that Jesus had come from Judea to Galilee, he went and begged Jesus to come to Capernaum to heal his son, who was about to die.

48 Jesus asked, "Will you never believe in me unless you see miraculous signs and wonders?"

⁴⁹ The official pleaded, "Lord, please come now before my little boy dies."

⁵⁰ Then Jesus told him, "Go back home. Your son will live!" And the man believed what Jesus said and started home.

⁵¹ While the man was on his way, some of his servants met him with the news that his son was alive and well. ⁵² He asked them when the boy had begun to get better, and they replied, "Yesterday afternoon at one o'clock his fever suddenly disappeared!" ⁵³ Then the father realized that that was the very time Jesus had told him, "Your son will live." And he and his entire household believed in Jesus. ⁵⁴ This was the second miraculous sign Jesus did in Galilee after coming from Judea (John 4:46–54 NLT).

What question does Jesus ask when the man comes to him (see verse 48)? What does this tell you about Jesus' intent in performing the healing for this man?

4. How did the man respond to Jesus' instructions (see verse 50)? How can waiting on God increase our faith? On the other hand, how can increased faith help us wait on God?

5. Have you ever experienced an increase in your faith when you were waiting on something? Or perhaps a strengthening of your character? Explain.

6. If you are waiting on God for something right now, what might be the purpose of your waiting? Write down your thoughts below.

Prayer: *Identify what you need most during those times when you are waiting for God to act. Do you need more faith, patience, hope? Ask God to give you those things today. End your time by contemplating or reading aloud these words from Psalm 130:5–6: "I wait for the* LORD, *my soul waits, and in His word I do hope. My soul waits for the Lord more than those who watch for the morning—yes, more than those who watch for the morning"* (NKJV).

AFTER BETHESDA

In your group time this week, you also looked at the story of Jesus healing the man by the Pool of Bethesda. The story reveals that sometimes it's easier (and more comfortable) to just stay stuck in a situation. The unknown of what life will look like after the change can be scary. And when you do get unstuck, sometimes others aren't happy about it. Maybe they are still stuck themselves or have another reason for not being supportive. The man by the pool of Bethesda experienced this, as the following account relates:

> [15] The man went away and told the Jewish leaders that it was Jesus who had made him well. [16] So, because Jesus was doing these things on the Sabbath, the Jewish leaders began to persecute him. [17] In his defense Jesus said to them, "My Father is always at his work to this very day, and I too am working." [18] For this reason they tried all the more to kill him; not only was he breaking the Sabbath, but he was even calling God his own Father, making himself equal with God (John 5:15–18).

1. If you knew a man who had been sick for thirty-eight years and then was miraculously healed, what would your response be? How did the Jews respond to the man's healing when he told them about it? Why were the Jews angry at Jesus?

2. Have you ever experienced a miracle in your life, but the people around you were not as excited about it as you? Why do you think that was? How did it make you feel?

3. Jesus' message was radical for the Jews of his time. He was claiming to be the Messiah, sent from God. He was claiming God was his father. This would have been a big deal to adherents of Judaism who took God's name seriously and revered him greatly. The Jews were experiencing what we all experience at times: *the threat of change.* Even if it's good change, it's natural for us to want to protect ourselves when our lives are shaken up. Do you feel resistant to change in your life right now? Particularly a change that could make you unstuck from a certain situation? If so, why do you feel resistant? Do you worry what others will think if you allow this change to happen?

4. John goes on to record the following words from Jesus in response to the persecution the Jewish leaders began to level at him for healing the man on the Sabbath:

[36] "I have testimony weightier than that of John. For the works that the Father has given me to finish—the very works that I am doing—testify that the Father has sent me. [37] And the Father who sent me has himself testified concerning me. You have never heard his voice nor seen his form, [38] nor does his word dwell in you, for you do not believe the one he sent. [39] You study the Scriptures diligently because you think that in them you have eternal life. These are the very

Scriptures that testify about me, [40] yet you refuse to come to me to have life" (John 5:36–40).

Of what was Jesus accusing his fellow Jews in this passage?

5. How is it possible to study Scripture but miss what Jesus is offering us?

6. According to Jesus, where is eternal life found (see verse 40)?

Prayer: *What are you struggling with today when it comes to change? Are you resisting taking actions that will make you unstuck? Do the people around you not support the fact you have experienced the love of Christ and are now unstuck from something? Are you judging a friend, family member, or loved one for the changes they have made in their lives? Wherever you find yourself today, bring that struggle honestly before God in prayer.*

SMALL BUT MIGHTY CHANGES

John relates in the opening chapter of his Gospel how Jesus called Andrew and Peter to follow him and become his disciples (see John 1:35–42). Luke relates some additional details in his Gospel about that encounter . . . when the two fishermen were feeling particularly stuck:

[1] One day as Jesus was standing by the Lake of Gennesaret, the people were crowding around him and listening to the word of God. [2] He saw at the water's edge two boats, left there by the fishermen, who were washing their nets. [3] He got into one of the boats, the one belonging to Simon, and asked him to put out a little from shore. Then he sat down and taught the people from the boat.

[4] When he had finished speaking, he said to Simon, "Put out into deep water, and let down the nets for a catch."

[5] Simon answered, "Master, we've worked hard all night and haven't caught anything. But because you say so, I will let down the nets."

[6] When they had done so, they caught such a large number of fish that their nets began to break. [7] So they signaled their partners in the other boat to come and help them, and they came and filled both boats so full that they began to sink.

[8] When Simon Peter saw this, he fell at Jesus' knees and said, "Go away from me, Lord; I am a sinful man!" [9] For he and all his companions were astonished at the catch of fish they had taken, [10] and so

were James and John, the sons of Zebedee, Simon's partners.

Then Jesus said to Simon, "Don't be afraid; from now on you will fish for people." [11] So they pulled their boats up on shore, left everything and followed him (Luke 5:1–11).

1. How did Peter respond to Jesus' request to "put out into deep water" and let down the nets (see verses 4–5)? Why was he reluctant to follow this request?

2. Peter and the others had been fishing all night, so it could be assumed they had also put out into deep water and let down their nets. Regardless of this, why do you think that Peter agreed to do what Jesus asked?

3. What happened when the fishermen followed Jesus' instructions?

4. Have you ever made a small change in your life that made a big difference? If so, what did you do? What inspired you to make the change? How did it affect your being stuck?

5. Think again about an area of your life where you are currently feeling stuck. What small change could you make in this situation?

6. What does this story tell you about the importance of being obedient to God even in the small things in life?

Prayer: *Read this prayer aloud or silently to yourself: "God, help me in the areas where I feel stuck in life. I don't always know how to get unstuck, what to change, or what the first step toward change even is. Show me the small things I can do now that will make a big difference in my life, in my heart, and in my relationships. Give me ears to hear and eyes to see so that I can follow in the way of Jesus and not stay stuck forever. Thank you for loving me where I am and thank you for loving me too much to leave me there. In Jesus' name I pray, amen."*

FURTHER REFLECTION

Use the space below to further reflect on what you studied this week: waiting on God, what happens after you're stuck, and the power of making small changes. Journal your thoughts or write them as a prayer to God, either asking him questions about what you learned, thanking him for what you learned, or seeking answers from him on what to do next now that you better understand these topics in Scripture. Also write down any observations or questions that you want to bring to your next group time.

For Next Week: In preparation for next week, read chapters 5–6 in *You Are Never Alone*.

God Is with You in the Storm

*A strong wind was blowing and the waters grew rough.
When they had rowed about three or four miles, they saw Jesus
approaching the boat, walking on the water; and they were
frightened. But he said to them, "It is I; don't be afraid."*

JOHN 6:18–20

WELCOME

We marvel at rainbows for a reason. They are a stunning sight in the sky, and they represent the calm that follows the storm. But a rainbow is the last thing we are thinking about in the *middle* of a storm. We're just trying to get through it, or out of it, or away from it. During difficult storms in life, it is easy to become so focused on the problem—whatever is causing the storm—that we miss what is happening in the midst of it.

In today's study, we will look at two more miracles of Jesus that John relates in his Gospel. The first involves Jesus feeding 5,000 men plus women and children, and the second involves him safely delivering the disciples from a raging storm on the Sea of Galilee. These miracles prove two things: (1) Jesus is with us in the storm, and (2) he knows how to get us out of it.

Both truths are critical when enduring hardship. Hardship blinds us, making it difficult for us to see a way out or experience the presence of Christ. Jesus can solve our problems. But he also wants us to know he is with us in the midst of them, not only when they are over.

Think about your closest relationship. Perhaps it is with a spouse or an old friend. What has made you closer over the years? What has made your relationship last this long? Chances are you have both endured trying times together and made it out on the other side. Did this weaken or strengthen your relationship? The fact you didn't abandon each other in the midst of the hardship likely means it strengthened your relationship.

It is the same with Christ. He is not just there to be your problem-solver. He does not only show up in the rainbow or the light at the end of the tunnel. He is there to weather the storm right there with you as you are going through it. Storms strengthen relationships. Jesus isn't going anywhere when one hits. Instead, he is as near as ever.

As you study these miracles, ask yourself where Jesus might be in your storm. Have you sensed his presence recently? Or have you been too focused on the problem? Jesus can lead you out of your storm. But he also wants you to know you are never alone in the midst of it.

SHARE

Begin your group time by asking anyone to share his or her insights from last week's personal study. Then, to get things started, discuss one of the following questions:

- When you are going through a difficult time, are you a glass-half-full or a glass-half-empty kind of person? Explain.

— or —

- When you are going through a stormy season in life, where do you tend to turn for comfort?

READ

Invite someone to read the following passage aloud. Listen for fresh insights as you hear the verse being read, and then discuss the questions that follow.

[16] When evening came, his disciples went down to the lake, [17] where they got into a boat and set off across the lake for Capernaum. By now it was dark, and Jesus had not yet joined them. [18] A strong wind was blowing and the waters grew rough. [19] When they had rowed about three or four miles, they saw Jesus approaching the boat, walking on the water; and they were frightened. [20] But he said to them, "It is I; don't be afraid." [21] Then they were willing to take him into

the boat, and immediately the boat reached the shore where they were heading (John 6:16–21).

What is one key insight that stands out to you from this passage?

At what point did Jesus appear to the disciples? What does this tell us about Jesus' presence in our own storms?

WATCH

Play the video segment for session three. As you watch, use the following outline to record any thoughts or concepts that stand out to you.

Jesus had crossed the sea to get away from the crowd. He needed time to grieve the loss of John the Baptist. But his love for the people quickly overcame his need for rest.

Philip saw no way to help "so many" in the crowd. Andrew wilted under the pressure of "so many." We can't really fault them. After all, we do the same.

It's not for us to tell Jesus our gift is too small. He can use what we have—and see us through the storm until we reach the other side.

The disciples must have felt abandoned. "Surely Jesus will help us," they thought. For six long hours, they fought the storm and sought the Master.

Before Jesus stilled the storm, he came to his friends in the storm.

If you're currently in a storm, think about the disciples' experience. Yes, you want this squall to pass and the winds to still. But above all, you want to know the great I AM is near.

DISCUSS

Take a few minutes with your group members to discuss what you just watched and explore these concepts in Scripture.

1. The day that Jesus performed the miracles of feeding the 5,000 and walking on the water had dawned with the news that John the Baptist had been killed by King Herod. King Herod had also sent word he wanted to kill Jesus next. How does this context affect the way you view the miracles Jesus performed? What does this say about who Jesus is?

2. How did Andrew and Philip respond to Jesus' question, "Where shall we buy bread for these people to eat?" (John 6:5). Do you think you would have responded to Jesus this way? Why or why not?

3. What represents "so many" in your life right now? Bills, relational problems, questions about your faith? How does this make you feel? How does it affect your everyday life?

4. What happened to the boy's offering in this story of Jesus feeding the 5,000? How could this bring hope to your own story of "so many"?

5. Jesus performed two different miracles in the midst of storms on the Sea of Galilee. Read Mark 4:35–41. How does this miracle differ from the one you heard about today?

6. In the story told in John's Gospel, even though the storm had not been calmed yet, how do you think the disciples felt when they realized the man walking on water was Jesus?

7. The name Jesus used to announce himself was the same one that God used in the Old Testament: *I AM*. What is the significance of Jesus' calling himself by this name?

8. Have you ever felt peace in the *midst* of a storm in your life—not when the storm was over—but in the middle of it? What caused this peace?

CLOSE

Close this session with an extended time of prayer together with your group. Break up into groups of two to share prayer requests and pray for one another. Then come back together as a group and use the following questions as a guide to spend a few moments in silence. One person can ask these aloud to the group, or you can work through them individually in silence.

- When was the last time you experienced the presence of Jesus in your life?
- Looking back on the past few days, can you identify a moment when Jesus was present?
- How might Jesus be present in whatever storm you are currently facing? What is he saying to you?
- How could Jesus' presence be helpful to you during this time?

End your time with one person praying aloud for the group to experience the presence of Jesus in a great way as you go about your week.

Between-Sessions
Personal Study

Reflect on the material you've covered this week by engaging in any or all of the following between-sessions activities. Each personal study consists of several reflection activities to help you implement what you learned in the group time. The time you invest will be well spent, so let God use it to draw you closer to him. At your next meeting, share any key points or insights that stood out to you as you spent this time with the Lord.

WHAT IS ENOUGH?

In this week's group time, you studied the miracle of Jesus feeding 5,000 men plus women and children with a few loaves of bread and fish. What seemed far from enough to feed a crowd ended up being enough to feed an army. You probably know what it feels like to not have enough time, money, patience, in your own life. It's easy to feel as if you just don't have enough to meet your needs, which begs the question: *What is enough?*

1. What do you feel you do not have enough of in your life right now? What *would* be enough of whatever you feel short on?

2. We often read the story of Jesus feeding the 5,000 as a story of abundance. Jesus miraculously produced an abundance of food, and we hope he will produce an abundance in our lives . But what if we read this story as a lesson in *contentment*? What if Jesus wanted us to know what we have in him is enough? Read John's account of this story again and answer the questions that follow.

   5 When Jesus looked up and saw a great crowd coming toward him, he said to Philip, "Where shall we buy bread for these people to eat?" 6 He asked this only to test him, for he already had in mind what he was going to do.

   7 Philip answered him, "It would take more than half a year's wages to buy enough bread for each one to have a bite!"

   8 Another of his disciples, Andrew, Simon Peter's brother, spoke up, 9 "Here is a boy with five small barley loaves and two small fish, but how far will they go among so many?"

¹⁰ Jesus said, "Have the people sit down." There was plenty of grass in that place, and they sat down (about five thousand men were there). ¹¹ Jesus then took the loaves, gave thanks, and distributed to those who were seated as much as they wanted. He did the same with the fish.

¹² When they had all had enough to eat, he said to his disciples, "Gather the pieces that are left over. Let nothing be wasted." ¹³ So they gathered them and filled twelve baskets with the pieces of the five barley loaves left over by those who had eaten (John 6:5–13).

How many barley loaves and fish were there? How much did everyone in the crowd end up getting to eat? When did the disciples stop serving the food?

3. This miracle proves the adage, "a little goes a long way." What is an example of this in your life? (It could be with tangible materials like money or food or with intangible things such as love and patience.) Explain your answer.

4. Why do you think it is so tempting to want more than you actually need? Realistically, what do you *need* more of in your life today? What do you actually have enough of?

5. Have you ever received more of what you needed, but then wanted more on top of it? For example, you got a raise . . . but wanted more money? Or you got a house . . . but then you decided you wanted a bigger one? If so, why did you then want more?

6. What does this miracle say about contentment? How can you apply this model of contentment to what you feel you are lacking today?

Prayer: *Spend your prayer time today expressing gratitude to the Lord. Write down a list of what you are thankful for that he has provided. Thank him for each item on this list, and then pray for an attitude of contentment so you can focus on what you have rather than what you want.*

RIDING OUT THE STORM

During a storm, the natural instinct is to seek shelter. But sometimes that isn't possible. Like the disciples on the Sea of Galilee, there are times when you find yourself with no choice but to ride out the storm. The money simply doesn't appear. The relationship doesn't get righted. The illness doesn't just go away. At such times, the only way out of the storm is through it. Perhaps this is why Jesus performed this miracle on this sea—to show he was *with* the disciples as they rode out the storm. In the same way, you can know that he will be present as you ride out your storm.

1. How do you typically weather the storms in your life? What are your coping mechanisms for hard times? Are your coping mechanisms effective? Why or why not?

2. It's easy to view the Bible as a book that contains magical solutions to problems, but if you look closely, there are fewer solutions than there are suggestions for getting through the hard times. The point of our faith isn't to use it to *avoid* pain but rather to use it as a help *during* pain. We see this clearly in the book of Psalms, which is a collection of poems that not only praise God but also express the writers' anguish, pain, and confusion. The

Psalms beautifully depict what it's like to be in the middle of a storm, as the following clearly relates:

[1] As the deer pants for streams of water,
    so my soul pants for you, my God.
[2] My soul thirsts for God, for the living God.
    When can I go and meet with God?
[3] My tears have been my food
    day and night,
while people say to me all day long,
    "Where is your God?"
[4] These things I remember
    as I pour out my soul:
how I used to go to the house of God
    under the protection of the Mighty One
with shouts of joy and praise
    among the festive throng.

[5] Why, my soul, are you downcast?
    Why so disturbed within me?
Put your hope in God,
    for I will yet praise him,
my Savior and my God.

[6] My soul is downcast within me;
    therefore I will remember you
from the land of the Jordan,
    the heights of Hermon—from Mount Mizar.
[7] Deep calls to deep
    in the roar of your waterfalls;
all your waves and breakers
    have swept over me.

⁸ By day the LORD directs his love,
at night his song is with me—
a prayer to the God of my life.

⁹ I say to God my Rock,
　　"Why have you forgotten me?
Why must I go about mourning,
　　oppressed by the enemy?"
¹⁰ My bones suffer mortal agony
　　as my foes taunt me,
saying to me all day long,
　　"Where is your God?"

¹¹ Why, my soul, are you downcast?
　　Why so disturbed within me?
Put your hope in God,
　　for I will yet praise him,
　　my Savior and my God (Psalm 42:1–11).

Underline any descriptions of pain the psalmist uses. What do these descriptions tell you about what the psalmist was going through and what he was feeling?

3. Now underline all the questions the psalmist asks. Of these questions, do any resonate with questions you are asking or have asked during a storm? If so, which ones?

4. Now underline the hopeful passages in this psalm where the psalmist praises God or seems to break through his pain. Why do you think the psalmist was able to have hope and praise God even in the midst of such terrible pain?

5. Notice how the psalmist's emotions seem to change from verse to verse. Why do you think this is the case?

6. How does this back-and-forth of emotion accurately reflect stormy seasons of life?

Prayer: *Identify where you are in your stormy season. Are you feeling deep in pain, or are you able to praise God and find hope? Wherever you are is okay. The psalmist in the passage you read today was honest with God about his questions and feelings. So be honest with God as well. Tell him where you are. Praise him if you are able. Or ask him some hard questions that have been on your mind. If it's helpful, use this psalm as a guide for your prayer time.*

THE GREAT I AM

When Jesus was walking toward the disciples in the storm, he identified himself as "I AM" (see John 6:20 NLT). It was a name God had been using since the story of Moses and the burning bush in the book of Exodus—a title of steadiness and power. This is significant, because Jesus was announcing his identity and his godly power to the disciples. If you pay attention, he will announce the same as you go through your storms in life.

1. As noted above, the first time God calls himself "I AM" occurs when he is talking with Moses at the burning bush. God gives Moses the responsibility of delivering the Israelites from slavery. Read the following account of this meeting and answer the questions below.

> [10] So now, go. I am sending you to Pharaoh to bring my people the Israelites out of Egypt."
>
> [11] But Moses said to God, "Who am I that I should go to Pharaoh and bring the Israelites out of Egypt?"
>
> [12] And God said, "I will be with you. And this will be the sign to you that it is I who have sent you: When you have brought the people out of Egypt, you will worship God on this mountain."
>
> [13] Moses said to God, "Suppose I go to the Israelites and say to them, 'The God of your fathers has sent me to you,' and they ask me, 'What is his name?' Then what shall I tell them?"
>
> [14] God said to Moses, "I AM WHO I AM. This is what you are to say to the Israelites: 'I AM has sent me to you'" (Exodus 3:10–14).

How did Moses respond to God's calling to deliver the Israelites out of Egypt (see verse 11)? How did God respond to Moses' hesitation (see verse 12)?

2. The phrase "I AM" in verse 14 uses the same Hebrew verb in verse 12, when God says, "I will be with you." God was telling Moses the one who has called him is the one who is with him. How beautiful that God has written the promise to be with us into his very name! What do you think God wanted Moses to understand in this passage about who he was and who Moses was?

3. In a way, Moses was also in a storm. He had been told he would be the one to lead this miraculous feat of delivering the Israelites, but he didn't know how it could be done. If you continue to read Moses' story, he went through many storms as his people wandered in the desert. But all the while, he had the promise of I AM. In a difficult time, it is natural to ask, *"When and how will this end?"* But what if instead you asked, *"Who is God in this time?"* How would asking that question change your outlook?

4. Think about what you have learned about Jesus so far through studying his miracles. What qualities does Jesus have that would make his presence comforting during a storm?

5. The name I AM is a symbol of steadiness and power. What promise do you need most today—Jesus' steadiness or his power? Why?

6. Whether you are in the middle of a storm, the beginning of one, or a storm is finally behind you, how will you invite I AM to be with you where you are today?

Prayer: *Read this prayer silently or aloud: "God, thank you for your promise to be with me. Thank you for your promise of I AM. Help me to cling to this promise today. Help me to see who you are clearly even in the midst of this storm that has made my life far from clear. Reveal your character to me and show me how to trust you more. May my heart look more like yours when this storm is over. I say this all in the name of Jesus, who came to embody the I AM. Amen."*

FURTHER REFLECTION

Use the space below to further reflect on what you studied this week: contentment, how to ride out a storm, and the promise that "I AM" will be with you in every trial. Journal your thoughts or write them as a prayer to God, either asking him questions about what you learned, thanking him for what you learned, or seeking answers from him on what to do next now that you better understand these topics in Scripture. Also write down any observations or questions that you want to bring to your next group time.

For Next Week: In preparation for next week, read chapter 7 in *You Are Never Alone*.

God Is with You in the Dark

They turned again to the blind man, "What have you to say about him? It was your eyes he opened." The man replied, "He is a prophet." . . . A second time they summoned the man who had been blind. "Give glory to God by telling the truth," they said. "We know this man is a sinner." He replied, "Whether he is a sinner or not, I don't know. One thing I do know. I was blind but now I see!"

JOHN 9:17, 24–25

WELCOME

If you are a believer, you probably remember the moment you accepted Christ. Recall that time now. Where were you? What did you feel and experience? What was your life like after you came to Jesus as compared to what it had been like before?

When you experience the love of Christ for the first time, it can feel as if you are seeing for the first time. Colors are more vivid . . . the trees, sky, and sound of birds more beautiful. Jesus' love changes us, and it changes how we see the world, ourselves, and others. This is because Jesus is our light and our life. As John wrote, "In him was life, and that life was the light of all mankind. The light shines in the darkness, and the darkness has not overcome it" (1:4–5).

The darkness is powerful and comes in many forms: *guilt, sin, trauma, anxiety, fear.* When you are in Christ, it's not that you will *never* experience these things again. Rather, in the midst of them, you will have the light of hope and healing. You will view the darkness in a new way—as something that is temporary, that does not define you, and from which you are safe.

Unfortunately, even the most religious among us can still be held captive by darkness if we have not received the freedom of Christ. This week, you will look at a miracle that John relates in which Jesus gave sight to a blind man. Although the feat was truly miraculous, the most religious of the group—the Pharisees—were not impressed. The reason is because they were themselves blind . . . not physically but *spiritually.*

Perhaps you will see a part of yourself in these characters, either in the Pharisees or the blind man who experienced the healing touch of Christ. Perhaps you will be reminded of the moment you first saw when you accepted Christ. Or perhaps that moment is still to come for you. Either way, keep your eyes open. Don't miss what Jesus has to offer you.

SHARE

Begin your group time by asking anyone to share his or her insights from last week's personal study. Then, to get things started, discuss one of the following questions.

- If you are already a Christ-follower, do you remember the moment you believed in Jesus? Did it affect how you saw the world or yourself?

— or —

- Have you ever had a dark place in your life that was healed by Jesus? What was it like to see that darkness turn to light?

READ

Invite someone to read the following passage aloud. Listen for fresh insights as you hear the verses being read, and then discuss the questions that follow.

[1] In the beginning was the Word, and the Word was with God, and the Word was God. [2] He was with God in the beginning. [3] Through him all things were made; without him nothing was made that has been made. [4] In him was life, and that life was the light of all mankind. [5] The light shines in the darkness, and the darkness has not overcome it.

[6] There was a man sent from God whose name was John. [7] He came as a witness to testify concerning that light, so that through him all might believe. [8] He himself was not the light; he came only as a witness to the light.

[9] The true light that gives light to everyone was coming into the world (John 1:1–9).

What is one key insight that stands out to you from this passage?

How are each of us—like John the Baptist—witnesses to the light of Jesus?

WATCH

Play the video segment for session four. As you watch, use the following outline to record any thoughts or concepts that stand out to you.

The disciples didn't really see the man. At least, not in the way that Jesus saw him. Rather, they just asked, "Rabbi, who sinned, this man or his parents, that he was born blind?" (John 9:2).

We often wonder if Jesus sees us in our plight. Does he understand our pain? Will he guide us when we can't see the way forward? John's story reveals the answer is *yes*.

Why was the man sightless? So that "the works of God might be displayed in him" (John 9:3). If we follow our troubles to the headwaters, we won't find a wrathful or befuddled God standing there. But we will find a *sovereign* God. Our pain has a purpose.

The man received sight not because he deserved it, earned it, or found it but because he obeyed the One who was sent to "open eyes that are blind" (Isaiah 42:7).

Sadly, some choose to remain blind to the work that God is doing in their midst. In this case, it was the religious leaders in the man's own community who chose to remain blind.

If you believe in Jesus, he has given you this pledge: "No one can steal [you] out of my hand" (John 10:28 NCV). Apart from Christ we are all like the blind man beside the road. But Jesus finds us, applies his miracle mud to our eyes, and guides us out of the darkness.

DISCUSS

Take a few minutes with your group members to discuss what you just watched and explore these concepts in Scripture.

1. Have you ever felt spiritually blind to something— whether blind to Christ himself, blind to a sin area in your life, or blind to the power of God? If so, what moment, person, or experience helped you see more clearly?

2. What question did the disciples pose to Jesus when they first saw the blind man on the road? Why do you think they asked this question? What was Jesus' response?

3. What do you think about Jesus' reasoning that sometimes we have hardships or ailments in order to bring glory to God? Have you experienced this in your life or know someone who has? If so, how has God been glorified in this difficult circumstance?

4. It couldn't have been pleasant for the man to have Jesus streak saliva-soaked mud on his eyes. But be forewarned: God still uses less-than-pleasant remedies today to help us see. Have you ever had to undergo a difficult remedy to see something that God wanted to show you? If so, what was the remedy? What were you able to see as a result?

5. Why did Jesus choose to heal the blind man? What did the blind man have to do to receive it? What lesson can you take away from this story?

6. Not everyone was impressed with Jesus healing the blind man. How did the Pharisees treat the man? Why do you think they responded this way?

7. Have you ever experienced something similar—someone in your life not understanding or believing in the hope you have in Jesus? What was that experience like for you?

8. What did Jesus do when he discovered the man born blind had been cast out of his community? What hope does this give you in your own life?

RESPOND

If you wear glasses or contacts, you know what a difference those vision-enhancements can make . . . and you can only imagine what it would be like to naturally have 20/20 vision. Spend some time in your group brainstorming what it would look like to have 20/20 *spiritual* vision. What would you know and understand? How would this vision affect your behavior, your relationships, your thoughts, and your attitudes?

CLOSE

Use the notes you captured above in your response time as a list of prayer requests. Have one person pray through the list for the group, asking God to give you eyes to see his will, his love, and his grace—20/20 spiritual vision.

Between-Sessions
Personal Study

Reflect on the material you've covered this week by engaging in any or all of the following between-sessions activities. Each personal study consists of several reflection activities to help you implement what you learned in the group time. The time you invest will be well spent, so let God use it to draw you closer to him. At your next meeting, share any key points or insights that stood out to you as you spent this time with the Lord.

BLINDED BY RELIGION

As you discussed this week, though the man born blind was miraculously healed by Jesus, not everybody was happy about it. Similar to the miracle story from session two, when Jesus healed the paralytic by the pool of Bethesda, the religious leaders were not pleased by the blind man's sudden sight. Read the following passage and answer the questions below.

¹⁴ Now the day on which Jesus had made the mud and opened the man's eyes was a Sabbath. ¹⁵ Therefore the Pharisees also asked him how he had received his sight. "He put mud on my eyes," the man replied, "and I washed, and now I see."

¹⁶ Some of the Pharisees said, "This man is not from God, for he does not keep the Sabbath."

But others asked, "How can a sinner perform such signs?" So they were divided (John 9:14–16).

1. Why were the Pharisees upset about this miracle (see verse 16)?

2. The Sabbath, or day of rest, was important to those who followed Jewish law. When Jesus made clay for the blind man's eyes, what he was doing was equivalent to kneading dough, which was one of thirty-nine acts forbidden on the Sabbath. Still, what Jesus did was remarkable. How does this story reveal the Pharisees had missed the point?

3. The Bible talks about the importance of the state of our hearts over our behavior. In Psalm 51:16–17, we read, "You do not delight in sacrifice, or I would bring it; you do not take pleasure in burnt offerings. My sacrifice, O God, is a broken spirit; a broken and contrite heart you, God, will not despise." What does God really want from us?

4. Jesus said, "Woe to you, teachers of the law and Pharisees, you hypocrites! You are like whitewashed tombs, which look beautiful on the outside but on the inside are full of the bones of the dead and everything unclean. In the same way, on the outside you appear to people as righteous but on the inside you are full of hypocrisy and wickedness" (Matthew 23:27–28). According to Jesus, what makes someone a hypocrite? Why wasn't Jesus impressed with the Pharisees' whitewashed exterior?

5. What do these verses say about how you are to follow God? What do they say about how you are to know if someone is a follower of God?

6. Jesus' miracles accomplished what God said he was going to do: "Therefore once more I will astound these people with wonder upon wonder" (Isaiah 29:14). How do miracles and wonders get us out of our religious heads and into our spiritual hearts?

Prayer: *As you saw today, sometimes our heads can get in the way of our hearts when it comes to our faith. A good way to get back in touch with the things of the heart and get out of your head is by getting into your body. At your prayer time today, do something physical, such as going on a walk, stretching in your living room, or taking a bike ride. As you move, talk to God. Be honest about the state of your faith—is it blinded by religion or open to the experiences Jesus has for you? When you're finished, be still and notice how this prayer time felt compared to others that you have had in the past.*

JESUS SEES YOU

One of the most beautiful parts of the story of Jesus healing the blind man is when Jesus goes after him at the end. The now-seeing man was shunned by his synagogue, community, and parents. In a moment of what must have been pure loneliness for the man, Jesus appears before him, proving that he does indeed see us in our plight. Read the post-miracle story that John records in his Gospel and then answer the questions below.

> [35] Jesus heard that they had thrown him out, and when he found him, he said, "Do you believe in the Son of Man?"
>
> [36] "Who is he, sir?" the man asked. "Tell me so that I may believe in him."
>
> [37] Jesus said, "You have now seen him; in fact, he is the one speaking with you."
>
> [38] Then the man said, "Lord, I believe," and he worshiped him.
>
> [39] Jesus said, "For judgment I have come into this world, so that the blind will see and those who see will become blind" (John 9:35–39).

1. The fact that Jesus heard "they had thrown him out" (verse 35) indicates he and his disciples had already left the area and continued on their way. Jesus could have considered his work finished, but he came back when he heard of the man's plight. What does his concern for the once-blind man say about how Jesus feels about you?

2. According to this passage, what did Jesus want the man to know? What does this tell you about the way in which Jesus heals people?

3. Have you ever wondered if God sees you? Perhaps you are wondering that now. What makes you doubt whether or not God knows what you are going through in your life?

4. God has many Hebrew names in the Bible that define his character. *El Shaddai* is God Almighty. *Rafa* is the God Who Heals. *El Roi* is the God Who Sees. The origin of this name is found in Genesis 16, when an enslaved woman named Hagar fled from Abraham and Sarah, because Sarah had dealt harshly with her. An angel of the Lord appeared to Hagar in the wilderness where she had fled and gave her a promise:

> [11] "You are now pregnant
> and you will give birth to a son.
> You shall name him Ishmael,
> for the Lord has heard of your misery.

^{12} He will be a wild donkey of a man;
    his hand will be against everyone
    and everyone's hand against him,
and he will live in hostility
    toward all his brothers "(Genesis 16:11–12).

In response, Hagar called the one who spoke to her, "You are the God who sees me" (Genesis 16:13). Often, when we see God, we realize he sees us. Describe a situation in your life when you found this to be true.

5. What is a struggle in your life that you wonder if God sees or cares about? Have you looked for God in this struggle? Why or why not?

6. Think about a time when you've struggled in the past. In hindsight, can you identify where God was or how God was working during this time? If so, explain.

Prayer: *Call on El Roi today, the God Who Sees, by reading this prayer silently or aloud: "El Roi, you are the God who sees me. Even though I know this, sometimes I wonder if you really see me and if you really care about me. Some areas of my life feel so difficult. I wonder if things will ever get better and doubt you are at work in that part of my life. Today, I do not want to doubt. I want to call on you, El Roi, the God who sees me. See my pain and hurt. See my heart and my regrets. May I see you as you see me. May I feel seen and as I feel seen, may I feel known. Thank you for making this possible through your son Jesus Christ. In his name I pray, amen."*

THE REMEDY

As you've seen, Jesus is our healer, but that doesn't mean the healing is always easy and carefree. Healing for our physical bodies requires medicine and recovery time. Often, we will feel pain before we feel better. The same is true of spiritual healing. Sometimes we have to go through something difficult or uncomfortable before we find ourselves on the other side. God will often use these less-than-pleasant remedies to help us see. Jesus offered the blind man a strange remedy in the miracle you studied this week. Read the following passage from John's Gospel and answer the questions that follow.

> ⁶ After saying this, he spit on the ground, made some mud with the saliva, and put it on the man's eyes. ⁷ "Go," he told him, "wash in the Pool of Siloam" (this word means "Sent"). So the man went and washed, and came home seeing (John 9:6–7).

1. What do you think the blind man thought when he heard Jesus spitting into his hands? How do you think the mud felt on his eyes?

2. How would being blind make this experience different than if the man could see what Jesus was doing?

3. What do you think the blind man thought would happen if he washed in the pool of Siloam?

4. Why did the man obey Jesus even though he didn't know who Jesus was?

5. Have you ever experienced a difficult, confusing, or messy remedy to receive spiritual healing? If so, why do you think that remedy was necessary?

6. In Psalm 119:105, we read, "Your word is a lamp for my feet, a light on my path." In the Old Testament, God's "word" referred to the law written by Moses. For believers in Christ, the "Word" refers to Jesus himself. How is Jesus—the "Word" and light-bringer—guiding you on the path he wants you to follow right now?

Prayer: *Honestly talk with God today about what you learned in this study. You could thank him for a remedy he gave you in the past or ask him questions about one you are undergoing today. Be honest. God wants your whole heart.*

FURTHER REFLECTION

Use the space below to further reflect on what you studied this week: the dangers of religion, being seen by God, and unlikely remedies. Journal your thoughts or write them as a prayer to God, either asking him questions about what you learned, thanking him for what you learned, or seeking answers from him on what to do next now that you better understand these topics in Scripture. Also write down any observations or questions that you want to bring to your next group time.

For Next Week: In preparation for next week, read chapter 8 in *You Are Never Alone.*

God Is with You in the Valley

*Jesus said to her, "I am the resurrection and the life.
The one who believes in me will live, even though they die;
and whoever lives by believing in me will never die.
Do you believe this?"*

JOHN 11:25–26

WELCOME

What comes to mind when you consider death? It's probably not a topic you are *dying* to think about, but it is nevertheless important. Have you experienced the death of loved ones in your life? Have you come to terms with your own? Or do you avoid it and try to numb yourself to its reality? It's true that the surest fact in life is also the one we fear the most: *death*.

However, if you're a believer, you have a sense of what it is like to be dead and now live. You know what it is like to move about this earth being a slave to your sin, guilt, and regret, and then meet Christ on the road. Suddenly, your life is filled with grace, peace, and a sense of forgiveness. This is the transition of death to new life. And it happens to be Jesus' specialty.

Jesus' miracles are all amazing—healing, turning water to wine, making a blind man see—but the miracle of Lazarus is perhaps the most awe-inducing. In this miracle, Jesus actually raised a dead man to life. And he didn't do so immediately after the man had died. He raised Lazarus after he had been dead for *four days*. There can be no mistake the man's heart had stopped beating and his breath had ceased. Jesus raised a man from death to life.

Don't miss the metaphor. Jesus didn't do this simply to amaze us. Rather, it speaks to his ability to raise each of us. His desire is to move us from a life of darkness and death to one that is vibrant with life. He wants to redeem us and forgive us of even the worst of sins that we have committed. This is why the cross parallels the miracle of Lazarus so beautifully. One proves Christ's victory over death. The other proves Christ's victory over our individual sin.

As we will see in this week's study, no miracle is more personal to each of us than the one that occurred when Jesus finally said, "It is finished" (John 19:30).

SHARE

Begin your group time by asking anyone to share his or her insights from last week's personal study. Then, to get things started, discuss one of the following questions:

- Have you ever considered Jesus' death on the cross as a miracle? Why or why not?

— *or* —

- What is your understanding of what happened on the cross? What was accomplished?

READ

Invite someone to read the following passage aloud. Listen for fresh insights as you hear the verses being read, and then discuss the questions that follow.

[21] "Lord," Martha said to Jesus, "if you had been here, my brother would not have died. [22] But I know that even now God will give you whatever you ask."

[23] Jesus said to her, "Your brother will rise again."

[24] Martha answered, "I know he will rise again in the resurrection at the last day."

[25] Jesus said to her, "I am the resurrection and the life. The one who believes in me will live, even though they die; [26] and whoever lives by believing in me will never die. Do you believe this?"

[27] "Yes, Lord," she replied, "I believe that you are the Messiah, the Son of God, who is to come into the world" (John 11:21–27).

What is one key insight that stands out to you from this passage?

Martha was able to profess her belief in Jesus as the Messiah even this soon after her brother, Lazarus, had died. Why do you think her belief in Jesus was still strong in this moment?

WATCH

Play the video segment for session five. As you watch, use the following outline to record any thoughts or concepts that stand out to you.

Jesus promised, "Lazarus's sickness will not end in death" (John 11:4 NLT). It would have been easy for the messenger to misunderstand the statement and believe Lazarus would not face death. Lazarus *would* find himself in the valley of death. But he would not stay there.

"Do you believe?" It's the same question Jesus asks us when we find ourselves in the middle of the valley of death. When all hope seems lost and Jesus' help seems missing.

No matter how well you run this race, you will not run it forever. When that time comes, you need Jesus' help to enter your eternal home. Thankfully, that help has already been given. For the raising of Lazarus was only a small hint of the greater resurrection to come.

It is finished. In the Greek, the phrase is a single word: *tetelestai.* It is a holy word. A sacred point in time. The moment the artist steps back from the canvas and lowers his brush. This announcement on Calvary was sufficient to save all who believe in him from eternal death.

The work of Christ on the cross satisfied the demands of the eternal tribune—the greatest of the miracles John records in his Gospel. Humanity had been *redeemed.*

Our part is to simply receive this great miracle of mercy—to let God's grace flow over us like a cleansing cascade, flushing out all dregs of guilt and shame. Nothing can separate us from God.

DISCUSS

Take a few minutes with your group members to discuss what you just watched and explore these concepts in Scripture.

1. What tends to be your reaction when you think about death and the end of your own life? Why do you think you react this way?

2. Read John 11:21–27. What promises did Jesus make to Martha in this passage? How did Martha respond to this promise from Christ?

3. Why do you think Jesus allowed Lazarus to die before he went back to Bethany?

4. How were the witnesses affected by seeing Lazarus raised from the dead? How did this accomplish Jesus' purpose that the miracle would result in bringing God glory?

5. The phrase *"it is finished"* is a single word in the Greek: *tetelestai.* What is significant about this word? What does it tell us about what Jesus accomplished on the cross?

6. In the Old Testament, the firstborn of every Israelite family legally belonged to God. However, he allowed each family to reclaim or "redeem" their firstborn child by paying a price. How did God do the same for us by allowing Jesus to die on the cross?

7. Paul wrote, "God made him who had no sin to be sin for us, so that in him we might become the righteousness of God" (2 Corinthians 5:21). How would you describe what this means? How are we made righteous through Jesus' death on the cross?

8. Remember the question that Jesus posed to Martha: "Do you believe?" (John 11:26). It's the same question Jesus asks us when we find ourselves in the middle of the valley of death. How would you answer this question today?

CLOSE

Close this session with an extended time of prayer with your group. Break up into groups of two and share prayer requests with one another. If you are comfortable in doing so, share any areas in which you are struggling with belief right now. Pray together to have the same kind of belief in Christ that Martha did, who said to the Lord, "I have always believed you are the Messiah, the Son of God, the one who has come into the world from God" (John 11:27 NLT).

Between-Sessions
Personal Study

Reflect on the material you've covered this week by engaging in any or all of the following between-sessions activities. Each personal study consists of several reflection activities to help you implement what you learned in the group time. The time you invest will be well spent, so let God use it to draw you closer to him. At your next meeting, share any key points or insights that stood out to you as you spent this time with the Lord.

WHAT HAPPENS WHEN YOU DIE?

Talking about death is an uncomfortable topic. But talking about death in the context of Christianity is different. This is because Jesus brings us hope in the face of our greatest unknown: the end of our lives. So, what does the Bible really say about what happens after death? Read the following passages in today's personal study to find out.

Death Isn't Final

1. A consistent theme in Scripture is that death isn't the end of the story. As Jesus said to his disciples in the following passage:

> [1] "Do not let your hearts be troubled. You believe in God; believe also in me. [2] My Father's house has many rooms; if that were not so, would I have told you that I am going there to prepare a place for you? [3] And if I go and prepare a place for you, I will come back and take you to be with me that you also may be where I am. [4] You know the way to the place where I am going" (John 14:1–4).

Why does Jesus say the disciples do not need to be troubled about death? What does he say that he is preparing for them?

2. What other promises does Jesus make in this passage to those who choose to follow him and put their faith in him as their Savior?

Jesus Will Be with You

3. Although we are not given all of the details about what heaven will be like, one fact is consistent in Scripture: Jesus will be there. As the apostle Paul writes:

> [6] Therefore we are always confident and know that as long as we are at home in the body we are away from the Lord. [7] For we live by faith, not by sight. [8] We are confident, I say, and would prefer to be away from the body and at home with the Lord (2 Corinthians 5:6–8).

What does Paul say about our current separation from the Lord? What does it mean to "live by faith, not by sight"?

4. In what does Paul say we can be confident? When will we be present with the Lord?

Jesus Will Be with You for Eternity

5. The Greek word *aionios* is used sixty-eight times in the New Testament. It means "without beginning and end, that which always has been and always will be." English translations render the word *aionios* as *eternity*, as the following passage relates:

> [16] Therefore we do not lose heart. Even though our outward man is perishing, yet the inward man is being renewed day by day. [17] For our light affliction, which is but for a moment, is working for us a far more exceeding and eternal weight of glory, [18] while we do not look at the things which are seen, but at the things which are not seen. For the things which are seen are temporary, but the things which are not seen are *eternal* (2 Corinthians 4:16–18 NKJV).

What is the difference between our "outward man" and "inward man"?

6. How could the definition of *aionios*—"without beginning and end, that which always has been and always will be"— help you understand the concept of eternity?

Prayer: *Read this prayer silently or aloud: "Father, you are the God of life and light. Death does not discourage you. You are not bound by time. You have been and always will be. My human brain has difficulty understanding the concept of death and heaven and eternity. Sometimes it makes me feel afraid. Sometimes it makes me hopeful. Sometimes I avoid thinking about it all together. Today, I give you all of my concerns, doubts, and fears surrounding death. I pray for peace in my spirit and hope in my heart. I pray for understanding, and when I don't have understanding, I pray for the peaceful presence of Christ. Thank you that death is not the end of my story and that in Christ, I can spend eternity with you. In his name I pray, amen."*

WHICH MARTHA ARE YOU?

If you've been a believer for some time, you have noticed your faith has evolved. It's grown, it's changed, and it's not exactly how it was when you first believed. As you discussed during the group time this week, Martha exhibited a strong faith when confronted with the death of her brother. Yet she wasn't always portrayed that way in Scripture, as the following account relates:

> [38] As Jesus and his disciples were on their way, he came to a village where a woman named Martha opened her home to him. [39] She had a sister called Mary, who sat at the Lord's feet listening to what he said. [40] But Martha was distracted by all the preparations that had to be made. She came to him and asked, "Lord, don't you care that my sister has left me to do the work by myself? Tell her to help me!"

⁴¹ "Martha, Martha," the Lord answered, "you are worried and upset about many things, ⁴² but few things are needed—or indeed only one. Mary has chosen what is better, and it will not be taken away from her" (Luke 10:38–42).

What was Martha's state of mind during Jesus' visit to her home? What did she ask Jesus to do? What did Jesus want her to do instead?

1. Overall, what is the tone of Martha's conversation with Jesus?

2. Now reread the conversation Martha had with Jesus after her brother died:

²⁰ When Martha heard that Jesus was coming, she went out to meet him, but Mary stayed at home. ²¹ "Lord," Martha said to Jesus, "if you had been here, my brother would not have died. ²² But I know that even now God will give you whatever you ask."
²³ Jesus said to her, "Your brother will rise again."
²⁴ Martha answered, "I know he will rise again in the resurrection at the last day."

^{25} Jesus said to her, "I am the resurrection and the life. The one who believes in me will live, even though they die; ^{26} and whoever lives by believing in me will never die. Do you believe this?"

^{27} "Yes, Lord," she replied, "I believe that you are the Messiah, the Son of God, who is to come into the world"(John 11:20–27).

Martha again comes to Jesus with what seems like a complaint—"if you had been here, my brother would not have died" (verse 21)—but she follows it with another statement. What is that statement? How is this different from the way she approached Jesus in the previous story (see Luke 10:40)?

3. Martha could have simply said "yes" when Jesus asked if she believed in him. But she chose to declare who Jesus is: "I believe that you are the Messiah, the Son of God, who is to come into the world." How does this show her faith had grown?

4. What is the overall tone of Martha's conversation with Jesus in this passage? How does it differ from the conversation she had with Jesus in Luke 10?

5. If you've been a Christian for some time, what has changed about your relationship with Christ over the years? What, if anything, is lacking in your communication with Jesus right now? What is strong in your communication with him?

Prayer: *Spend some time in prayer before the Lord, talking to him about whatever is on your mind. As you pray, notice the tone you take, your posture, and the state of your conversation with him. Ask that he will continue to help you to grow in your faith and trust in him.*

"YOU INTENDED TO HARM ME . . ."

Throughout this study, you've seen glimpses of the dislike the Pharisees had of Jesus' miracles, but when Christ raised Lazarus from the dead, their dislike morphed into hate. Even though Jesus and the Pharisees were both Jews and part of the same community in Israel, the Pharisees would ultimately betray him into the hands of the Romans.

1. Have you ever been betrayed by someone in your our "tribe" or community? If so, how did that person betray you? How did you respond to the betrayal?

2. The Pharisees began to plot against Jesus in earnest after they heard about Lazarus' resurrection, as the following passage from John relates:

45 Therefore many of the Jews who had come to visit Mary, and had seen what Jesus did, believed in him. 46 But some of them went to the Pharisees and told them what Jesus had done. 47 Then the chief priests and the Pharisees called a meeting of the Sanhedrin.

"What are we accomplishing?" they asked. "Here is this man performing many signs. 48 If we let him go on like this, everyone will believe in him, and then the Romans will come and take away both our temple and our nation."

49 Then one of them, named Caiaphas, who was high priest that year, spoke up, "You know nothing at all! 50 You do not realize that it is better for you that one man die for the people than that the whole nation perish."

51 He did not say this on his own, but as high priest that year he prophesied that Jesus would die for

the Jewish nation, [52] and not only for that nation but also for the scattered children of God, to bring them together and make them one. [53] So from that day on they plotted to take his life (John 11:45–53).

3. Why were the Pharisees concerned about Jesus? What action did they ultimately decide to take to remove the threat that Christ posed to them?

4. John notes the Pharisees claim that Jesus' growing number of followers would cause the Roman authorities to retaliate against them. Caiaphas, the high priest, suggested sacrificing Jesus in order to save the rest of the Jews. However, the idea of sacrificing one for many was not a Jewish value. In fact, Jewish tradition taught the opposite—to not betray a single Israelite, even if that meant others would perish. So, if Jesus wasn't *actually* a threat to the Jews in this way, why do you think the

Pharisees wanted to kill Jesus? What was the real reason why they wanted to put Jesus to death?

5. The Pharisees' plot against Jesus was ultimately successful. It came about as a result of another betrayal—from one of his own disciples—and led to the Romans arresting him in the Garden of Gethsemane. John relates the moments of Christ on the cross:

25 Near the cross of Jesus stood his mother, his mother's sister, Mary the wife of Clopas, and Mary Magdalene. 26 When Jesus saw his mother there, and the disciple whom he loved standing nearby, he said to her, "Woman, here is your son," 27 and to the disciple, "Here is your mother." From that time on, this disciple took her into his home.

28 Later, knowing that everything had now been finished, and so that Scripture would be fulfilled, Jesus said, "I am thirsty." 29 A jar of wine vinegar was there, so they soaked a sponge in it, put the sponge on a stalk of the hyssop plant, and lifted it to Jesus' lips. 30 When he had received the drink, Jesus said, "It is

finished." With that, he bowed his head and gave up his spirit (John 19:25–30).

Jesus' statement, "It is finished," was not a surrender but a declaration of victory. Humanity had been *redeemed*. How does this represent the greatest miracle in the gospel? How do you respond to this act of redemption—of Jesus taking on your sin so you would never have to be separated from God?

6. In the Old Testament, we read how Joseph was betrayed by his brothers and sold into slavery in Egypt, where he suffered greatly. Yet when he looked back on his life, he could say to them, "You intended to harm me, but God intended it for good to accomplish what is now being done, the saving of many lives" (Genesis 50:20). How does this statement apply to Jesus and the Pharisees' plot against him? How does it apply to you?

Prayer: *Personalize Genesis 50:20 in your prayer time today. Replace "you" with the name of the person who hurt you, and then thank God for the good that came of it. If there is any hurt or pain left from the betrayal, bring that before the Father. Ask him to help you forgive the person who hurt you or take whatever steps are necessary to move toward healing.*

FURTHER REFLECTION

Use the space below to further reflect on what you studied this week: what happens after we die, how we communicate with Jesus, and how God can use evil for good. Journal your thoughts or write them as a prayer to God, either asking him questions about what you learned, thanking him for what you learned, or seeking answers from him on what to do next now that you better understand these topics in Scripture. Also write down any observations or questions that you want to bring to your next group time.

For Next Week: In preparation for next week, read chapters 10–12 in *You Are Never Alone*.

God Is with You When You Need Grace

When they had finished eating, Jesus said to Simon Peter, "Simon son of John, do you love me more than these?" "Yes, Lord," he said, "you know that I love you." Jesus said, "Feed my lambs."

JOHN 21:15

WELCOME

If you are a dog owner, you've experienced your pet's shame when he or she does something wrong. Maybe you walk into the house after being out for the evening, and the first thing you see are pieces of your couch cushion chewed up. Or the cake on the counter is mysteriously missing. Instead of greeting you at the door, your dog is off cowering in a corner, awaiting his punishment, ashamed of what he has done.

Humans aren't much different when we make mistakes. Our instinct is to run and hide . . . to avoid the call, the apology, the text. But shame will never heal us. At some point, confession, repentance, and restoration are needed. In the end, we find that even though the steps toward restoration were difficult, the restoration was completely worth it.

Jesus well understands our human failings. Although his disciples spent nearly every moment with him during his time on earth, they were certainly not perfect as he was. They messed up frequently. Judas betrayed him into the hands of the Pharisees. Peter denied three times that he even knew Christ. The rest of the disciples abandoned Jesus at the cross.

The disciples also had their failings when it came to Jesus' most staggering miracle—his resurrection from the grave. Most of them doubted. One of them refused to believe until he saw the evidence firsthand. One of them saw the empty tomb and *believed.* Regardless of their actions and reactions, Jesus still loved them. And displayed this love in an incredible way. He didn't add to their shame or punish them. Instead, he chose to be present with them after his resurrection. He was a safe place for them to confess, repent, and ultimately believe.

We all have similar failings as disciples. Yet the promise of the gospel is that no matter how much we doubt God, mess up, or fail, Jesus is ready to forgive us and be with us. He offers us the same gift as he offered to the disciples: *grace.*

When we are in Christ, we are truly never alone.

SHARE

Begin your group time by asking anyone to share his or her insights from last week's personal study. Then, to get things started, discuss one of the following questions.

- How do you typically react when you feel shame over something you have done? Do you think this is a healthy or unhealthy response? Explain.

— *or* —

- When is a time that you chose to extend grace to another person who had wronged you? What happened as a result of your gift?

READ

Invite someone to read the following passage aloud. Listen for fresh insights as you hear the verses being read, and then discuss the questions that follow.

¹⁵ Simon Peter and another disciple were following Jesus. Because this disciple was known to the high priest, he went with Jesus into the high priest's courtyard, ¹⁶ but Peter had to wait outside at the door. The other disciple, who was known to the high priest, came back, spoke to the servant girl on duty there and brought Peter in.

¹⁷ "You aren't one of this man's disciples too, are you?" she asked Peter.

He replied, "I am not."

¹⁸ It was cold, and the servants and officials stood around a fire they had made to keep warm. Peter also was standing with them, warming himself. . . .

²⁵ So they asked him, "You aren't one of his disciples too, are you?"

He denied it, saying, "I am not."

²⁶ One of the high priest's servants, a relative of the man whose ear Peter had cut off, challenged him, "Didn't I see you with him in the garden?" ²⁷ Again Peter denied it, and at that moment a rooster began to crow (John 18:15–18, 25–27).

What is one key insight that stands out to you from this passage?

What events related in this passage led up to Peter's denial of Christ?

WATCH

Play the video segment for session six. As you watch, use the following outline to record any thoughts or concepts that stand out to you.

John had not understood when Jesus said "it is finished" that he was declaring his mission to be completed. In fact, for him and the rest of the disciples, it looked like everything was finished in a difference sense. For them, it seemed like the *end*.

John entered Jesus' tomb and saw the evidence. He did the math: the stone rolled away, the now-tenantless tomb, the linens in their original state. Only one explanation made sense: *Jesus himself had done this!* John saw and *believed*.

Peter had denied even knowing Christ when confronted about his association with Jesus. But now, Jesus was alive. How could he face his Master again after what he had done?

Peter had fallen publicly and personally. So Jesus restored him publicly and personally. Peter had denied him three times. So Jesus asked Peter three times if he loved him.

Jesus emerges as the hero in the story. But Peter still had to take his step. He answered. He obeyed. He responded. He interacted. He stayed in communion with Christ. Jesus turned a denying Peter into a proclaiming Peter. He did so then. He does still today.

The message of the miracles is the Miracle Worker himself. You are stronger than you think because God is nearer than you imagine. For when you belong to God, you are never without help, never without hope, and never without strength. Truly . . . *you are never alone.*

DISCUSS

Take a few minutes with your group members to discuss what you just watched and explore these concepts in Scripture.

1. Even though Jesus prepared the disciples for what would happen to him, they still abandoned him the night of his arrest and during his trial and crucifixion. Why do you think the disciples did this? What was motivating them?

2. Read John 20:1–10. At what point in this passage did John believe? What do you think caused him to believe?

3. We often say, "I have to see it to believe it." Are you this type of person? Or does faith come easily for you? Explain.

4. Peter had boldly cut off the ear of the high priest's servant when Jesus was arrested in the Garden of Gethsemane. Why do you think Peter so soon afterward denied even knowing Christ? In what ways can you relate to Peter's experience?

5. What is symbolic about the way Jesus restored Peter to himself? What does this say about Jesus' character? What does it say about his willingness to extend grace?

6. If the distance between Jesus and Peter consisted of a hundred steps, Christ took ninety-nine and a half. But Peter still had to take his step. What was that step that Peter had to take? What does this say about the part we play in our restoration?

7. Consider Peter's story in the context of your faith. Are you ashamed of any failure from your past that is keeping you from being in communion with God? Or ashamed of any doubts that you have? If so, what one step could you take toward Jesus today?

8. As you close this discussion time, what are one or two valuable truths you would like to share that you have learned in this study? What have you learned about yourself?

RESPOND

Use the space below to write down two or three goals that you believe would help strengthen your relationship with God and remind you that *you are never alone*. Break up into groups of two or three when you are finished to share together what you have written.

CLOSE

End your time by reading the following prayer aloud. One person can read, or you can all read together: "Dear God, thank you for this time of study together. Thank you for your Word. Thank you for Jesus. You have promised that we are never alone. Give us confidence in that promise. Remind us we are never alone in the ordinary moments of life, when we feel stuck, when we are in the storms and valleys, when we are in the dark, and even when we fail. You are with us in every moment, fear, and doubt. Thank you for your presence. Make us more aware of it each day. In Jesus' name, amen."

Final
Personal Study

Reflect on the material you've covered this week by engaging in any or all of the following final personal study activities. Each study consists of several reflection activities to help you implement what you learned in the group time. The time you invest will be well spent, so let God use it to draw you closer to him. Be sure to share with your group leader or group members in the upcoming weeks any key points or insights that stood out to you.

A SLOW AND STEEP CLIMB

John understood in writing about Jesus' resurrection that he was asking a lot for us to believe. He knew that we might have doubts when we read about the other miracles that he relates in his Gospel. But the resurrection? That was pushing it up a notch. Still, maybe it was for the best. We all need to work through our misgivings and ponder the truths about our faith. We need to seek out answers and ascend the steps—as slow and steep as the climb may be—that will take us to belief in Christ.

1. Have you ever had to work through misgivings about your faith or ponder the truths in the gospel? If so, what were you uncertain of that you needed to work through?

2. What uncertainties are you pondering now, even at the end of this study?

3. Doubt gets a bad rap in Christianity and faith communities. But if you look at the way doubts and questions are addressed in the Bible, they are not sinful or wrong. In fact, they seem to be a necessary part of the faith journey, not a detour from it. The following story in the Gospel of Mark illustrates how Jesus responds to our doubts:

> [17] A man in the crowd answered, "Teacher, I brought you my son, who is possessed by a spirit that has robbed him of speech. [18] Whenever it seizes him, it throws him to the ground. He foams at the mouth, gnashes his teeth and becomes rigid. I asked your disciples to drive out the spirit, but they could not."
>
> [19] "You unbelieving generation," Jesus replied, "how long shall I stay with you? How long shall I put up with you? Bring the boy to me."
>
> [20] So they brought him. When the spirit saw Jesus, it immediately threw the boy into a convulsion.

He fell to the ground and rolled around, foaming at the mouth.

²¹ Jesus asked the boy's father, "How long has he been like this?"

"From childhood," he answered. ²² "It has often thrown him into fire or water to kill him. But if you can do anything, take pity on us and help us."

²³ "'If you can'?" said Jesus. "Everything is possible for one who believes."

²⁴ Immediately the boy's father exclaimed, "I do believe; help me overcome my unbelief!"

²⁵ When Jesus saw that a crowd was running to the scene, he rebuked the impure spirit. "You deaf and mute spirit," he said, "I command you, come out of him and never enter him again."

²⁶ The spirit shrieked, convulsed him violently and came out. The boy looked so much like a corpse that many said, "He's dead." ²⁷ But Jesus took him by the hand and lifted him to his feet, and he stood up (Mark 9:17–27).

On the surface, this passage seems to contain conflicting messages about doubt. What tension or questions do you have about this story?

4. Notice Jesus' statements in verse 19. What do you think his tone was like when he asked the questions? Why did he feel this way?

5. Jesus tells the father, "Everything is possible for one who believes" (verse 23). What is the man's response to this statement? Can you relate to his sentiment? If so, how?

6. What does this story tell you about how Jesus responds to your doubt and unbelief? What hope does this give you as you work through your own doubts?

Prayer: *The father's words in this story are a perfect prayer in and of themselves: "I do believe; help me overcome my unbelief!" These words are enough to offer to God when you have doubts. Recite this verse today along with anything else you need to bring to God in prayer.*

NOT ASHAMED

In this week's group time, you discussed Peter's denying Christ and the shame he felt as a result. Numerous other characters in the Bible also experienced shame. In fact, shame is literally the oldest story in the book. In the opening chapters of Genesis, we read how God instructed Adam and Eve to not eat from the tree of knowledge of good and evil (see 2:15–17). So what did they do? They ate from the tree of knowledge of good and evil . . . and then hid from God. Here is how the Lord responded to their act:

> ⁸ Then the man and his wife heard the sound of the Lord God as he was walking in the garden in the cool of the day, and they hid from the Lord God among the trees of the garden. ⁹ But the Lord God called to the man, "Where are you?"
>
> ¹⁰ He answered, "I heard you in the garden, and I was afraid because I was naked; so I hid."
>
> ¹¹ And he said, "Who told you that you were naked? Have you eaten from the tree that I commanded you not to eat from?"
>
> ¹² The man said, "The woman you put here with me—she gave me some fruit from the tree, and I ate it."
>
> ¹³ Then the Lord God said to the woman, "What is this you have done?"
>
> The woman said, "The serpent deceived me, and I ate" (Genesis 3:8–13).

1. Why did Adam and Eve hide? Where did they hear God walking?

2. Why do you think God was looking for Adam and Eve?

3. What kind of conversation did God have with Adam and Eve? What did they tell God?

4. What is a recent example from your life where you made a mistake and had this instinct to hide from the one you hurt or let down? What happened as a result?

5. According to this story, where is God in our shame? How does he deal with our shame?

6. What do you feel shame about today? Where do you sense God in your shame?

Prayer: *Read this prayer aloud or silently to yourself: "Dear God, I know you are with me even in my shame. My shame and guilt make me want to run and hide, but today, I run to you. I bring you my shame, so you can take it away from me. This is why you sent your Son—so that I would never have to suffer the shame of sin again. In Christ, I am new, every day. Shame does not have to weigh me down. Thank you for this truth. In my Savior's name I pray, amen."*

THAT YOU MAY BELIEVE

John didn't record the miracles of Jesus to simply awe his readers. As he said, "These are written down so you will believe that Jesus is the Messiah, the Son of God, and in the act of believing, have real and eternal life in the way he personally revealed it" (John 20:31 MSG). Hopefully, your belief has been strengthened—or at least examined—during this study. In your final personal study time, return to session one in this study guide and read the answers and reflections you wrote down under the heading, "Do You Believe in Miracles?"

1. Look at what you wrote down in response to question 3: "How do you feel about the miracles described in the Bible? Do you believe they happened or do you consider them folklore?" Has your answer to this changed? Remained the same? Explain.

2. Review the six promises you've studied, beginning with *God is with you in the ordinary.* How have you experienced God in your everyday life in the last six weeks?

3. *God is with you when you're stuck.* What have you learned about how God can help you when you are stuck?

4. *God is with you in the storm and in the dark.* Where have you sensed God's presence in a storm that you have endured? How has God helped you see something new in an area of your life that was once dark?

5. *God is with you in the valley.* What have you learned about God as you consider "the valley of death"—either your own or that of a loved one? What hope have you gained in this study when you consider the fact of your own mortality?

6. *God is with you when you need grace.* Where has God met you in your shame? Where do you most need God's grace today? What one step do you need to take?

Prayer: *How do you feel as you end this study? Grateful? Peaceful? Confused? Maybe you have mixed feelings? Identify what you're feeling and bring that before God. Thank him, ask him whatever lingering questions you have, or simply sit in his presence.*

FURTHER REFLECTION

As you close this study, expound on what you wrote during your response time in this week's group session. Record any others goals you have set for yourself that were inspired by this study and how you hope to achieve them.

Leader's Guide

Thank you for your willingness to lead your group through this study! What you have chosen to do is important, and much good fruit can come from studies like this. The rewards of being a leader are different from those of participating. We hope that as you lead your group, you will find your own walk with Jesus deepened by this experience of learning about his miracles in the Gospel of John and what they mean for your life today.

You Are Never Alone is a six-session study built around video content and small-group interaction. As the group leader, imagine yourself as the host of a dinner party. Your job is to take care of your guests by managing all the behind-the-scenes details so that when everyone arrives, they can just enjoy time together.

As the group leader, your role is not to answer all the questions or reteach the content—the video, book, and study guide will do most of that work. Your job is to guide the experience and cultivate your small group into a kind of teaching community. This will make it a place for members to process, question, and reflect—not receive more instruction.

There are several elements in this leader's guide that will help you as you structure your study and reflection time, so follow along and take advantage of each one.

BEFORE YOU BEGIN

Before your first meeting, make sure the group members have a copy of this study guide so they can follow along and start reading if they desire to do so. Alternately, you can hand out the study guides at your first meeting and give the group members some time to look over the material and ask any preliminary questions. During your first meeting, be sure to send a sheet around the room and have the members write down their name, phone number, and email address so you can keep in touch with them during the week.

Generally, the ideal size for a group is between eight to ten people, which ensures everyone will have enough time to participate in discussions. If you have more people, you might want to break into smaller subgroups. Encourage those who show up at the first meeting to commit to attending the duration of the study, as this will help the group members get to know each other, create stability for the group, and help you know how to prepare each week.

Each of the sessions begins with an opening reflection. The two questions that follow in the "Share" section serve as an icebreaker to get the group members thinking about the topic at hand. You can choose which question you want to ask. Typically, one question is a little more in-depth, and one is more surface-level. Take the temperature of your group to decide which one you should discuss.

Note that some people may want to tell a long story in response to one of these questions, but the goal is to keep the answers brief. Ideally, you want everyone in the group to get a chance to answer, so try to keep the responses to a minute or less. If you have talkative group members, say up front that everyone needs to limit the answer to one minute.

Also, give the group members a chance to answer, but tell them to feel free to pass if they wish. With the rest of the study, it's generally not a good idea to have everyone answer every question—a free-flowing discussion is more desirable. However, with the opening icebreaker questions, you can choose to go around the circle. Encourage shy people to share, but don't force them.

At the end of session one, invite the group members to complete the between-sessions personal studies for that week. Explain that you will be providing some time before the video teaching next week for anyone to share insights. Let them know sharing is optional, and it's no problem if they can't get to some of the between-sessions activities some weeks. It will still be beneficial for them to hear from the other participants and learn about what they discovered.

WEEKLY PREPARATION

As the leader, there are a few things you should do to prepare for each meeting:

- *Read through the session.* This will help you to become familiar with the content and know how to structure the discussion times.

- *Decide which questions you definitely want to discuss.* Based on the amount and length of group discussion, you may not be able to get through all of the Bible study and group discussion questions, so choose four to five questions that you definitely want to cover.

- *Be familiar with the questions you want to discuss.* When the group meets, you'll be watching the clock, so make sure you are familiar with the questions you have selected. In this way, you'll ensure you have the material more deeply in your mind than your group members.

- *Pray for your group.* Pray for your group members throughout the week and ask God to lead them as they study his Word.

- *Bring extra supplies to your meeting.* The members should bring their own pens for writing notes, but it's a good idea to have extras available for those who forget. You may also want to bring paper and additional Bibles.

Note that in many cases there will be no one "right" answer to the question. Answers will vary, especially when the group members are being asked to share their personal experiences.

STRUCTURING THE DISCUSSION TIME

You will need to determine with your group how long you want to meet each week so you can plan your time accordingly. Generally, most groups like to meet for either ninety minutes or two hours, so you could use one of the following schedules:

SECTION	90 MINUTES	120 MINUTES
WELCOME (members arrive and get settled)	10 minutes	15 minutes
SHARE (discuss one or more of the opening questions for the session)	10 minutes	15 minutes
READ (discuss the questions based on the Scripture reading for the week)	10 minutes	15 minutes
WATCH (watch the teaching material together and take notes)	20 minutes	20 minutes
DISCUSS (discuss the Bible study questions you selected ahead of time)	30 minutes	40 minutes
RESPOND / PRAY (pray together as a group and dismiss)	10 minutes	15 minutes

As the group leader, it is up to you to keep track of the time and keep things moving according to your schedule. You might want to set a timer for each segment so both you and the group members know when your time is up. (Note there are some good phone apps for timers that play a gentle chime or other pleasant sound instead of a disruptive noise.)

Don't be concerned if the group members are quiet or slow to share. People are often quiet when they are pulling together their ideas, and this might be a new experience for them. Just ask a question and let it hang in the air until someone shares. You can then say, "Thank you. What about others?"

GROUP DYNAMICS

Leading a group through the *You Are Never Alone Study Guide* will prove to be highly rewarding both to you and your group members. However, this doesn't mean you will not encounter any challenges along the way. Discussions can get off track. Group members may not be sensitive to the needs and ideas of others. Some might worry they will be expected to talk about matters that make them feel awkward. Others may express comments that result in disagreements. To help ease this strain on you and the group, consider the following ground rules:

- When someone raises a question or comment that is off topic, suggest you deal with it another time, or, if you feel led to go in that direction, let the group know you will be spending some time discussing it.

- If someone asks a question you don't know how to answer, admit it and move on. At your discretion, feel free to invite group members to comment on questions that call for personal experience.

- If you find one or two people are dominating the discussion time, direct a few questions to others in the group. Outside the main group time, ask the more dominating members to help you draw out the quieter ones. Work to make them a part of the solution instead of the problem.

- When a disagreement occurs, encourage the group members to process the matter in love. Encourage those on opposite sides to restate what they heard the other side say about the matter, and then invite each side to evaluate if that perception is accurate. Lead the group in examining other Scriptures related to the topic and look for common ground.

When any of these issues arise, encourage your group to follow these words from the Bible: "Love one another" (John 13:34), "If it is possible, as far as it depends on you, live at peace with everyone" (Romans 12:18), "Whatever is true . . . noble . . . pure . . . lovely . . . if anything is excellent or praiseworthy—think about such things" (Philippians 4:8), and "Be quick to listen, slow to speak and slow to become angry" (James 1:19). This will make your group time more rewarding and beneficial for everyone who attends.

Thank you again for your willingness to lead your group. May God reward your efforts and dedication, equip you to guide your group in the weeks ahead, and make your time together in *You Are Never Alone* fruitful for his kingdom.

Endnotes

Page 16: "As discussed this week, the closest English translation of Jesus' words in John 2:4 appear to be, 'Mother, your concern and mine are not the same.'" Robert H. Mounce, *The Expositor's Commentary: John* (Grand Rapids, MI: Zondervan Academic, 2007) vol. 10, p. 387.

Page 64: "God was telling Moses the one who has called him is the one who is with him." Jeremy Royal Howard, ed., *HCSB Study Bible* (Nashville, TN, Holman Bible Publishers, 2010), p. 103.

Page 78: "When Jesus made clay for the blind man's eyes, what he was doing was equivalent to kneading dough, which was one of thirty-nine acts forbidden on the Sabbath." Craig S. Keener, *The IVP Bible Background Commentary: New Testament* (Downers Grove, IL: Intervarsity Press, 1993), p. 288.

Page 100: "The Greek word aionios . . . means 'without beginning and end, that which always has been and always will be.'" Ibid., p. 293.

Page 106: "In fact, Jewish tradition taught the opposite—to not betray a single Israelite, even if that meant others would perish." Ibid., p. 294.

NEW 40-DAY STUDY THROUGH ROMANS

The *40 Days Through the Book* series helps believers more actively engage with God's Word. Each study encourages you to read through one book in the New Testament during the course of 40 days and will provide you with (1) a clear understanding of the background and culture in which the book was written, (2) insights into key passages of Scripture, and (3) clear applications and takeaways.

In *Romans*, Max Lucado guides you through Paul's letter to the believers in the city of Rome, revealing what the Apostle's words meant to his original readers . . . and how they apply to us today.

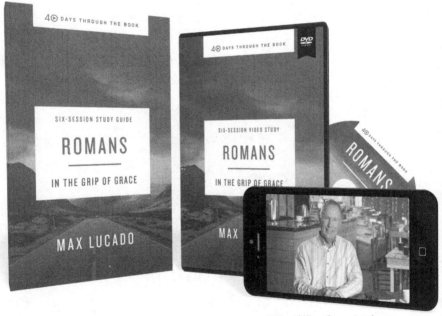

Study Guide
9780310126119

DVD with Free Streaming Access
9780310126133

Coming soon to your favorite bookstore,
or streaming video on StudyGateway.com.

Thomas Nelson
Since 1798

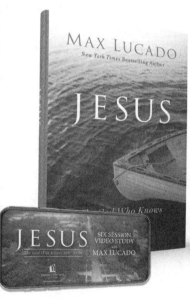
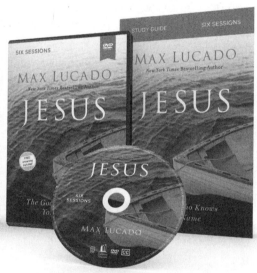

CELEBRATE EASTER, CHRISTMAS, AND THE LIFE AND MINISTRY OF JESUS

In *Because of Bethlehem*, a four-session video Bible study, Max Lucado explores how the One who made everything chose to make himself nothing and come into our world. Jesus' birth gives us the promise that God is always near us, always for us, and always within us—and that we no longer need to have marks on our record.

In *He Chose the Nails*, a five-session video Bible study, Max continues by examining the gifts that Christ gave at his crucifixion. These include not only the gift of the cross but also the gift of the thorns, the nails, and the empty tomb. The cross is rich with God's gifts of grace, and as we unwrap them, we will hear him whisper, "I did it just for you."

Book	Christmas Study Guide	DVD	Easter Study Guide	Book
9780849947599	9780310687054	9780310687849	9780310687269	9780718085070

Available now at your favorite bookstore,
or streaming video on StudyGateway.com.

THERE IS A PATH TO HAPPINESS THAT ALWAYS DELIVERS

In this book and video Bible study, Max Lucado shares the unexpected path to a lasting happiness, one that produces reliable joy in any season of life. Based on the teachings of Jesus and backed by modern research, *How Happiness Happens* presents a surprising but practical way of living that will change you from the inside out.

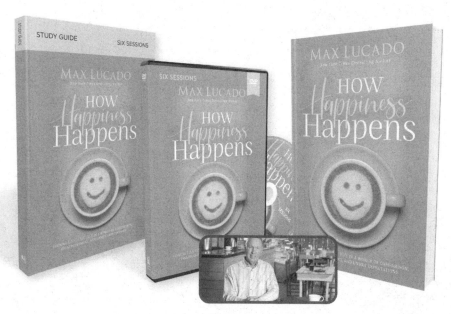

Study Guide
9780310105718

DVD with Free Streaming Access
9780310105732

Book
9780718096137

Available now at your favorite bookstore,
or streaming video on StudyGateway.com.

GOD HAS A CURE FOR YOUR WORRIES

Anxiety doesn't have to dominate life. Max looks at seven admonitions from the Apostle Paul in Philippians 4:4–8 that lead to one wonderful promise: "The peace of God which surpasses all understanding." He shows how God is ready to give comfort to help us face the calamities in life, view bad news through the lens of sovereignty, discern the lies of Satan, and tell ourselves the truth. We can discover true peace from God that surpasses all human understanding.

Study Guide	DVD	Softcover
9780310087311	9780310087335	9780718074210

Available now at your favorite bookstore,
or streaming video on StudyGateway.com.

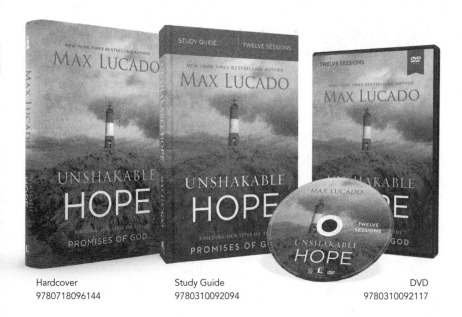

STUDY THE BIBLE BOOK-BY-BOOK WITH MAX LUCADO

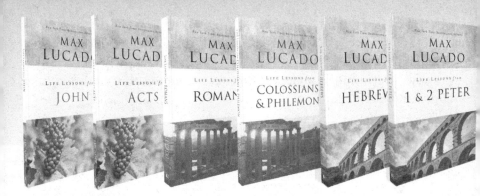

The *Life Lessons with Max Lucado* series brings the Bible to life in twelve lessons filled with intriguing questions, inspirational stories, and poignant reflections to take you deeper into God's Word. Each lesson includes an opening reflection, background information, an excerpt of the text, exploration questions, inspirational thoughts from Max, and a closing takeaway for further reflection. Ideal for use in both a small-group setting and for individual study.

Available now at your favorite bookstore.

THOMAS NELSON
Since 1798